wishing for snow

ALSO BY MINROSE GWIN

The Queen of Palmyra

A MEMOIR

wishing for snow

MINROSE GWIN

HARPER ● PERENNIAL

NEW YORK ● LONDON ● TORONTO ● SYDNEY ● NEW DELHI ● AUCKLAND

HARPER ● PERENNIAL

A hardcover edition of this book was originally published in January 2004 by Louisiana State University Press.

FIRST EDITION

Designed by Barbara Neely Bourgoyne

Library of Congress Cataloging-in-Publication Data
Gwin, Minrose.
Wishing for snow : a memoir / Minrose Gwin.
p. cm.
ISBN 978-0-06-204634-5

11 12 13 14 15   RRD   10 9 8 7 6 5 4 3 2 1

for Carol

I

Diary of Erin Taylor Clayton
DO NOT DISTURB

Friday November 21, 1930

Well I have started to school again as usal this morning. Mama called me her little sunshine. I realy do think I am helping her get over GranPapa being dead. I do hope I can altho I am so hurt my self. Well reccess is over and we have thought up a new game. I can't write any more right now because we are going to have a lesson so goodby for a little while. Gee Whiz! I have to stay in and I was just whispering. If Frances hadn't turned around Miss Olivo wouldn't have ever known I was whispering.

Monday November 24, 1930

I am writting a story! Boborae Stone is making up the names of the stories and I am writing them. She is helping me a little bit. I sure do hope it will snow tonight.

II

LAMENT

Already you begin to fade,
You who dreamed us
as we might have been:
Tonight I dream you
mother yet child again.
My child   anybody's child
one of those sad
incredibly wide-eyed waifs
shivering on the last cold shingle
of the world.

Go back now   I say   *go back*
it's too late
you are too heavy for me to hold.

ERIN CLAYTON PITNER

I am the daughter of the woman who wrote this poem. My
mother was born in the July heat of a Mississippi summer in
1921. Today is her birthday, the go-for-broke dive through the
swampy birth canal, my poor grandmother, her nerve endings
at fever pitch, setting her teeth. I imagine my still-young grandmother (Minrose the Latin teacher whose students always win
the state tournament, only thirty-one) propped on her elbows,

3

drenched from head to toe, swearing over her monstrous belly, as we all do in this moment, that this stubborn one will be her last. It is late afternoon, the time of day when overripe figs tremble and slip to earth without a sound. Some are so distended with nectar they crack and leak, drawing wasps and yellow jackets to straddle and sip.

My mother would be eighty this first day of July had she not left this life in transit. She died in the back of an ambulance summoned to the nursing home (ambulance attendants are known to call this The Hearse Run) where she spent her last days fewer than twenty miles from her birthplace, her own belly bloated with the poison fluids of reproductive cancer. Her wish for pencil and paper the main thing on her mind.

Fourteen years ago:

I drive into my carport to find two large boxes piled up next to the door. My first shipment from Mississippi after my mother's death. I open them right there on the carport and find my inheritance in pieces. A crystal bowl crushed into slivers. Two brass candelabra in chunks broken at the joints. A glass plate cracked in half. (Notably absent: items 4 and 5 on the list of items willed to me—an antique ring with seven diamonds and the family silver—both probably long gone to pay the doctors, the psychiatrists, the nice private institution, the grim state institution, and finally the nursing home; or perhaps just lost.)

These broken items have been packed with newspaper and the pillows from Mama's sofa. The satin throw pillows were once bright colors. My mother loved color and liked to give color new names. She called these "rusty apricot." Now the satin feels oily and damp. There are four of the pillows, and they smell like Mama's house in the last years. It's an odd smell, something I've never smelled anywhere else, not just the odor of decay, or the total absence in the house of anything remotely close to being clean, but the smell of the *misuse* of things — the meals eaten off good china in closets, a dark sweetness permeating sheets and towels and clothes and upholstery, the mysterious stains, a relish jar under every bed, each with its own fork laid, with practical intent I assume, a few inches to the left of the jar. Rotten meat. Other things I cannot speak of.

In those days there were things that were one thing and then became another, taking on the madness, making me jump and pant when I would find them behind doors or under furniture, scaring me to death when all they might be were just things, ordinary things. The hundreds of pieces of material cut into shreds and put in the same old white dirty clothes hamper I had put my dirty clothes in and my brother and sister put their dirty clothes in all of our child lives wherever we had lived. Or, arranged like an open fan on the closet floor with phone book and jars, dozens of pages of text Erin Taylor has hand copied from someone's scholarly book. (Later I will discover that it is my book she has copied word by word.) On each side of the closet floor a pleasant line of shoes, covered with lists in my mother's handwriting of people and their phone numbers, the beginning of a list of everyone she knows in town. The lists are, insofar as I can tell, functioning to keep the shoes clean. The jars, a greasy tattered telephone book, and a list of names like a party list or a Christmas card list: everyday things strangely transformed by usage or placement.

Now, the sickness has come to me in a box. It is in the pillows. I can smell it. I am not imagining this smell. My husband smells it too. He says nothing, but his face tightens, and without asking or being asked, he takes the pillows out to the storage shed in the backyard and throws them in with the lawn mower and rakes and fertilizer. At night I think about them lying there and pondering what is going to happen next in their strange lives as pillows.

After a few nights I begin to dream that they are unhappy. They want to be dry-cleaned. They want to come inside and lie on my couch. They are thinking they can toast themselves in front of the fire and look out the window. They are wanting us to rest our heads on them and take dreamy naps on hot summer afternoons, or throw them at each other in fun.

One night I dream that they are climbing over the lawn mower and working the lock to the shed. The next day I gather them up fast and throw them in the garbage can. For days I picture them there, wounded by this unseemly treatment, like cousins who knock at the door and are turned away for no good reason.

At 8:17 on Tuesday morning I am watching from behind my curtain for the garbage truck to round the bend in my street. I fully expect that there will be some accident, a spillage, and the pillows will make their getaway. Then, the clank of the truck making the bend and, before I can take a deep breath, the garbage men have picked them up and thrown them into the back of the truck. This, I feel, is a miracle of vast proportion.

By now they have rotted away in some overcrowded landfill on the side of a mountain in Virginia. I know that, as I write, they are no longer intact, they are no longer the place of the Bad Smell. As the months and years have rolled by, they have peacefully dissolved. They have lost my mother's smell and her stains.

❈ ❈ ❈

My mother was given the double name of Erin Taylor after her maternal grandmother, Erin Lee Taylor Kincannon, a woman not known for her gentleness or good luck, her husband Vann and one daughter both suicides by the less-than-neat method of a gun to the head, and another more fortunate daughter the president of a women's college Up North, her long-term living arrangements with a woman physician named "Doctor Patty" never discussed in public or private. One son, Vann Junior, after enlisting in the marines at age nineteen to do his share, according to the clipping in my grandmother's scrapbook, "in keeping the foot of the Hun off the sacred soil of America," became a newspaper reporter and then, either consecutively or simultaneously, a paregoric drinker and drug addict (what "drug addict" meant in those days is not clear; "drug fiend" was what he was called) immortalized in several sketches of Mississippi. As a girl, I would sit outside on my great-grandmother's front porch steps with Uncle Vann, who was even then skin and bones. (Something Had Happened to Him in the Great War, it was whispered, but no one knew what.) He'd be sipping paregoric and eating cloves to cover the smell. I used to sit leaning against his bony knees, chewing cloves and inhaling the kick from the small bottle he held hidden between cupped hands. A couple of decades later, I would rub paregoric on my baby daughter's gums (such things were then permissible, even advised). When she would quiet down, which she invariably did, I would lick the stuff off my fingers and find myself flooded with pleasure.

I remember the first Erin as an old woman in diapers who screamed at the women who changed them, their guarded faces averted from the bite of ammonia and, I think now, from the glare of her whiteness. "Miss Erin," as she was called by all, looked like a loaf of dough covered in a fine dust of flour, except when her toothless gums flashed in anger at the disturbance during these discrete changes of cloth diapers, which then had to be washed by hand and hung out to dry on the clothesline out back. The line always billowed with large white rectangles smelling of bleach. Miss Erin had white hair and she always wore starched white gowns that covered all but her old veiny feet and hands. She lay in a puddle of white sheets in her dark four-poster bed pushed up against the wall to prevent further fallings from above like the one that had put her there in the first place.

For Miss Erin, there had been seven children in all, including an eye surgeon ("a *noted* eye surgeon," my mother would say) and four more girls, one dying in childbirth after bringing into the world a man who would become a Green Beret and militant anti-Communist (who blighted my college years by bringing me trophies from the ROTC group he commanded, boys with tight pants, prominent chins, prickly heads, and yearnings for jungle combat; one jutted his chin out several times a minute like a twitchy cock at a cockfight). The youngest of Miss Erin and Vann Senior's children, Jane Stuart, did not marry until her thirties because she so enjoyed flirting, dancing, and being sought after. She was my mother's favorite aunt, though that's not saying much, since, of the four other possibilities, two were dead, one was a lesbian (the latter fate worse than the former), and one had married a missionary to the Belgian Congo and hadn't been seen since except in photos surrounded by uneasy-looking Africans. Jane Stuart carried her sense of herself as a belle of renown to her last nursing home, where, in her eighties, she giggled happily during the recreation hour, bouncing the beach ball when it came her way, a favorite of all the attendants.

Miss Erin was the granddaughter of William Henry Calhoun and Jane Stuart Orr of South Carolina (whose name was passed down to her southern belle great-granddaughter). It was a match. William was the nephew of John C. Calhoun and this first Jane Stuart the daughter of Governor Orr of South Carolina. Both of these forefathers were formidable. They knew their Cicero and used it in elaborate rhetorical defenses of the three big S's—Slavery, States' Rights, and Secession. The dark walnut dresser in my bedroom, which had been my great-grandmother's, grandmother's, and mother's before making what I then thought would be its longest and most irrevocable journey to me in New Mexico, was said to have been carried to Mississippi on a wagon pulled by, who knows, mules perhaps, along with William and Jane Stuart's other possessions, some of whom were doubtless men, women, perhaps even children who slogged those hundreds of miles—shoes, if there were any to start with, falling to shreds, bare feet first bleeding, then coating over like pine resin. I see their footsteps in sand, then pitchy mud, then red clay, alongside the wagon train of the adventuresome and well-supplied young couple from Carolina coming across first Georgia, then Alabama, then finally the new territory.

When the foot drags a bit to left or right, does it mean someone is thinking of home, though it is hard to say what home is, when folks are so here and there? (And who is thinking such a thing? Those who leave or those who come?) Gather wood and fix suppers over the fire. Save a bite of something back for the next day and the babies. Tumble into small clumps of weariness at day's end. Touch and touch again the raw line at the ankle.

The pulls on the old dresser drawers are hand carved to look like walnut shells but they actually look like breasts. The wood is dark. When the dresser was finally delivered to me after my stepfather's death, a small top drawer contained several rusty hat pins.

Even before she became an invalid, Miss Erin was said to be hard to please. People were afraid to bring her news she didn't want to hear. "Who is going to tell Miss Erin?" was always the first question after bad news. Perhaps she had already heard too much: the shot ringing out so unaccountably in that year of suicides, 1930, when Vann Senior, a salesman of drugs (did he bring home the pretty little bottles his son cupped so lovingly in his bony hands?), having lost all in the crash, decided to give it up altogether, blowing his brains out at his desk on the second floor of the white house wreathed in crepe myrtle.

What does one think in such a moment? Today one might think sonic boom, fireworks, a car backfiring, terrorism, almost anything but this, but Miss Erin must have known better. Perhaps she did not even run up those stairs; perhaps she just took off her apron and sat down by the window and looked out for a while before going next door to say help us, please help us.

More than two decades later, as a little girl barely able to walk I would venture over to Miss Erin's house many times; it was just a block down Church Street from my grandparents' home, and I would scuff along between the two houses with my cousins, up and down the sidewalks upended by the roots of the sweet gums and oaks. It shocked me several years ago to look at a photograph and see that Miss Erin's house had two stories because, in all my visits over the years, I had not seen anyone, no matter how crowded it got downstairs, ever climb the gleaming wood staircase, at the top of which the door was firmly shut. Everyone seemed to have forgotten there was an upstairs.

After Miss Erin's death, the gas company, like a vulture picking up a still-fleshy bone, bought and tore down the house, second story and all, and poured concrete for a parking lot.

NEW PARKING LOT

The tall grey house lies level
with the street.
The lawn is starkly white
taut with the shimmer
of well-laid concrete.
Cars crouch over the caged grass
their black bellies belching oil
on the graves of the flowers.
The dark bulbs stretch and crack
crying for light.
And I hear them
the daffodils
spearing through the sod
scrabbling beneath the concrete
screaming for the sun.

ERIN CLAYTON PITNER

Several years ago, in cleaning out my southern belle great-aunt's belongings from her dresser at the nursing home, I found two telegrams from her sister Bess, Erin and Vann Senior's daughter whose husband Jack, my grandmother would say in her schoolteacher's voice, wasn't worth a red cent, which was the harshest judgment my grandmother ever laid at anyone's door and which meant Jack was a mean drunk. The first telegram, dated March 30, 1947, read: HAVE BEEN PUT TO BED FOR MONTH WITH FRACTURED SKULL STOP SAY NOTHING TO JACK LET MOTHER THINK ACCIDENT CAUSED BY FALL BESS. The second, dated the next morning read: PRAY THIS IS SHOCK JACK NEEDED RESTING FAIRLY COMFORTABLE LOVE—BESS.

Bess too would, a few years hence, curl her short, blunt Kincannon forefinger around the coolness of metal and pull. She did so one day when her youngest of five boys was at school. I do not know what he found of his mother when he came home that afternoon, perhaps tired and hungry for one of those nice snacks mothers sometimes have waiting for hungry boys. *Mother* might have been on his lips when he first touched the front door, perhaps in a whisper because by then she had come to drink as much as her husband and he might have thought her napping. I hope she locked herself in the bathroom and pinned a note on the front door, in the old-timey way, a straight pin in and out of the screen, to say: "Son, dear, please do not come in. Go next door and tell them Mama is sick and they should send a doctor. Go straight on over there."

Afterward, his face took on an open look like someone who has been traveling long distances without sleep. He was always looking at a spot to the left or right of you until you would turn to see what it was he was looking at and find nothing at all. (My mother's suicide attempts were less determined. "Something must be wrong with the steering," she would say in a puzzled voice. "The car keeps running off the road. It just does.")

I have three pictures of Miss Erin. In the first, she looks about twenty. Her green blouse and the black ribbon around her neck, as well as her earrings, have been sketched onto the head, as was customary in old photographs. I see now how my mother looked very much like her, especially in the even but spacious curve of jaw from tip of chin to earlobe, though the young Miss Erin's eyes, unless they are painted falsely, were brown, while my mother's, her namesake's, were light, a gray blue. The mouth is the same, full, almost pursed as if something of importance, perhaps even a secret, is about to be told. In the other two pictures, Miss Erin is old, wearing the starched white cotton she finally took to her bed in. Behind her wire frames, her eyes look out benignly. Unlike in the earlier picture, in both of these she is smiling, as if pleased.

Even in the fleshiness of middle age, my mother looked nothing like her own mother (though who knows what the bones would say). Erin Taylor was the third and indeed final child of Minrose Kincannon Clayton, the sweet-faced teacher (Minrose's lips curved naturally up, even when she was angry) whose name and profession I have taken through this life and whose students did actually win the state Latin tournaments almost every year, on one glorious occasion all first, second, and third places. Minrose's husband and Erin Taylor's father was Stewart Philip Clayton, a lawyer and federal bankruptcy referee, a hymn-singing floor-walking Sunday School teacher who loved the idea of individual but not social justice and who, at his death in August of 1958, was said to be the oldest male native in what was then still a small southern town. Minrose, born a scant ten months after her parents' marriage in 1889, was named ingeniously, for two maiden aunts, Aunt Minnie ("actually Minerva, for wisdom," Aunt Minnie would say with a sniff) and Aunt Rose, who lived together like two cantankerous hens on the same nest and who, although inseparable, were covetous of each other's turns of good fortune, so much so that to have named the first baby girl—a golden egg for sure—for one or the other would have been unthinkable.

What the newspaper clipping in my grandmother's scrapbook says is that Miss Minrose Kincannon and Stewart Philip Clayton, Esq., were married in late September of 1911 after a series of delightful entertainments, including a Japanese party during which the guests left their shoes at the door, put on lovely kimonos, and were seated à la Japanese on mats. Little girls of the hostesses danced for the bride and groom on the veranda and rode in a tiny jinricksha pulled by costumed boys. One little costumed girl rode along carrying an armful of Japanese asters, each containing a good wish, and these were showered on the bride to be. Almost ninety years later, all mentioned in the yellowed clippings of my grandmother's scrapbook are now gone: the bride, the groom, their group of well-wishers in kimonos, the little Japanese girls and little Japanese boys (with last names like Robinson and McNabb and Grisham), even my mother, who was then only a hopeful ovum in my virginal grandmother's sweetly curving belly.

The December before, bride, groom, boys, and girls had had a delicious taste of mortality when A. Y. "Birdman" Moisant and his internationally famous traveling air show came to the Tri-County Fair, drawing a crowd of eight thousand from the countryside at large, directly after which Moisant, with his daredevil pilots, traveled to New Orleans. There, a few days hence on New Year's Eve, he fell from the sky in an aery ball of fire. Some old-timers would later say the accident actually might have happened at the fair, especially since it was looking like snow that day and nearly fogged in, and it almost seemed that it had, since the Birdman was dead before anyone had stopped dreaming about his crazy curlicues. Official photographs of him in goggles atop his aeroplane at the Tri-County Fair bear the scrawled epitaph, "Moisant was killed in New Orleans Dec. 31st 1910."

In the fall of 1911, though, as Minrose and Stewart's wedding came and went, townsfolk had little thought of death and time's passage. Everything seemed new. People up and down the streets were out on their front porches nailing boxes to their doors for the first free visit from the government mailman. Electric lights were going on all over town. The event of the season was indeed not this or any other wedding but the dramatic unveiling by the local Woman's Christian Temperance Union of a great brass woman with outstretched wings on an eight-foot pedestal. The flying woman, who guarded the west side of the courthouse square in the center of town, commemorated the adoption of statewide prohibition. In years to come, she would be called "The Temperance Lady," and her wings would shade Minrose's younger brother Vann and his drug fiend cohorts (certainly an exaggerated epithet for these gentle nodding fellows with their whiskery faces), who would sit on the courthouse steps and dreamily sip paregoric and other delectables from small brown sacks. Once, when my mother and I were downtown, we saw Uncle Vann sitting in his covey of friends on the courthouse steps. I tried to run over to greet him, but my tight-lipped mother jerked me back from the flock gathered under the Temperance Lady's friendly wings and led me protesting down the sidewalk in the other direction.

Minrose and Stewart's wedding was at four-thirty in the handsome new Presbyterian Church, beautifully arrayed in its garniture of green, with graceful ferns and waving palms presenting a lovely background to the enlivened scene. A Mrs. Price sweetly sang "Drink to Me Only with Thine Eyes" and "Oh! To Be Loved," and after a reception in the church basement, the happy couple left on the Frisco train for Memphis, Tennessee, where they remained throughout the week. In Minrose's bedroom for years to come would hang the framed verse:

> Married in September's golden glow
> Smooth and serene your lives will flow.

Minrose's scrapbook, which includes a poem to her alma mater, the first state-supported women's college in the country, old "I. I. & C." (Industrial Institute & College, where Minrose's mother Erin had gone through in the first graduating class and where Minrose herself was president of the senior class), later more appropriately named Mississippi State College for Women ("The W," which I attended for a couple of years and learned not to walk and smoke at the same time), still later Mississippi University for Women (still "The W," but now drawing some nice young men who wanted to be nurses), begins with an inscription in her handwriting of John Greenleaf Whittier's lines:

> I know not where His islands lift
> Their fronded palms in air;
> I only know I cannot drift
> Beyond his love and care.

The scrapbook ends abruptly with the announcement of "the arrival of a sweet girl baby at the home of Mr. and Mrs. S. P. Clayton" on the page opposite a recipe for curing meat:

Take a molasses barrel and make up a brine that will float an egg. Add a gallon of molasses and a little saltpetre. After the meat has the animal heat out of it place the hams and shoulders hock down in the barrel of brine. Place the middlings on top of the joints and above all place a weight that will keep the meat securely under the brine. Leave the meat undisturbed for six weeks and selecting some clear, dry day take it out, wipe it off thoroughly, dry and sprinkle rub thoroughly with borax. Hang and smoke.

This method is almost sure to save meat in the warmest weather if the animal heat is out of it when packed in the brine.

The sweet girl baby was not my mother, but her older sister Linda, after whom, in precise three-year intervals, came a boy, Stewart Junior, called "Boy Blue," and then, finally, my mother, who was born the same year they rebuilt Stewart's old family home on the corner of Church and Walnut Streets. The new house was a square two-story of red brick with only a sweeping covered porch, a large porch swing, and the intuition of motion both offered, to recommend it aesthetically. I do not know which came first, the birth of my mother or the completion of the stolid new house on the old foundation, but the two—the child and the house—must have been twinned in a peculiar way: Erin Taylor, the last baby, with those surprised eyes and an O for a mouth, sledding across the oiled floors, banging a tender baby elbow on the unscratched clay tile of the porch, curling fat fingers around a brass doorknob that shone not from polishing but from newness. (A fragment from one of my mother's poetry notebooks reads, "All she can see are feet, and she scuttles behind them.") It is no wonder that Erin Taylor would always think the house was hers, even when it was sold to Northerners who planted a monstrous pot that looked like a spaceship in the front yard. "A *red* pot," Mama would say, and her lip would curl.

The house's forebear, an angular frame dwelling which appears to have been added onto randomly, had been built in the 1890s by William Lafayette Clayton, called (of course) "the Colonel" though he was not one. This William, father of the floor-walking, night-wandering Stewart Senior and grandfather of little Erin Taylor, had come to frontier Mississippi in 1840 as a four-year-old boy from a place in northern Alabama called, proprietarily, Clayton's Grove. It was four years after the Chickasaws had had their loyalty to the United States rewarded by being removed from their tribal lands, not in one or two treaties written in a few sittings, as in the case of the Choctaw Nation's losses farther south, but over time in bits and nibbles. These Chickasaws, many of them by then of mixed blood, were sent on their way in dispirited and hardly noticeable bands of fifty to a hundred or so, leaving behind the mossy burial mounds one might expect and the huge plantation houses that must have been surprising in their opulence to a little boy from the hills of Alabama.

Well into his stern-faced, goateed sixties, this child pioneer William, who had occupied himself in adulthood first with the Civil War and then as a lawyer riding up and down the Natchez Trace carrying his papers arguing justice in dusty saddle bags, would write newspaper stories about the magnificent virgin forests of his youth with great uplifting and overtopping poplar, walnut, chestnut, hickory, oak, and gum trees as far as the eye could see. It was a matter of only a few years that the North Mississippi wilderness had been conquered by bull-tongue plow and whipsaw. The settlers had set about felling the great oaks along the old Natchez Trace, trees with trunks so wide that a dozen men could stand around them with arms outreached and still not touch, in forests where one could see miles away with nothing to obstruct the view but the massive trunks. Soon the settlers also dispatched the Carolina paroquets, large parrot-sized birds of brilliant red, orange, and green with large curved beaks, because they ate the grain. The Carolina paroquets were the easiest to kill of all the pests. When one of their number went down, they would all flutter around the fallen comrade in alarm and grief. Then they made easy targets, even for boys.

With the exceptions of a fall from a pony, which broke her shoulder, and a disastrous tornado—both of which occurred the year my mother turned fifteen—Erin Taylor ("Tatie," as her friends called her) grew up uneventfully in the red brick house—at least this is what I've been led to believe by everyone concerned. For the former, she was sent to "Employees' Hospital" in Fairfield, Alabama, according to the address I have on a letter she received from her teacher "Coach" Hinge, who offered to send the animal back to Egypt, Assyria, Jerusalem, or "some where over there" where horses came from, and congratulated her on her bravery. She lived with her parents and the older sister and brother in the house she had come to love with the long front porch where in the summers the cousins, neighbors, aunts, uncles would sit for hours in the big swing and rocking chairs, swatting mosquitoes and talking about the terrible state of the northern branch of the Presbyterian Church.

Sometimes, my mother said, Miss Alice Anderson, the blind lady next door to whom we were related by marriage, would throw open her French doors and raise her windows and play Rachmaninoff on her grand piano, and someone would tell Erin Taylor as the youngest to bring out a pitcher of sweet tea to cool them down. Then they would be satisfied. They would all sit on the porch and sip their tea and listen to the sound of those tortured chords (Miss Alice in her darkness never played anything soothing) crashing over the buzz of the katydids and the moan of the mosquito trucks moving up and down the streets in soft clouds of spray. In such moments the smells of insecticide and mimosa would seem indistinguishable.

The Great Tornado came on a yellow afternoon; Erin Taylor said you could feel it coming. The air was too hot and too thick to breathe and so utterly still that you thought anything, even a tornado, would be a relief. Under her cast—this wasn't long after the pony fall—my brave teenaged mother was on fire. She was pacing the front porch trying to get a bent coat hanger down under the cast while the sky burned.

She would tell it like movie frames:

I was itching like I'd gotten into red ants and I heard them call to me to come on and bring a jug of ice water. I got the water and went down those steep dark steps to the basement. The water sloshed over me, but it felt good. I remember it felt just right. Daddy was down there already, squatting on a pile of old papers. He had his nose stuck in *The Christian*

Observer, like everything was hunky-dory and this was the living room. Mama was fanning herself with an old straw fan she kept down there. The candles were burning and I could see the slop jar back in the corner. Nobody said anything. We were all listening. Just when I sat down on the stairs as close to the top as I could and pulled a cube of ice out of the pitcher to put down my cast, there's this roar a freight train makes coming through the upstairs, then a high-pitched sound like a siren. The whole house is caving in on us it sounds like. Windows bursting like there's a war going on and we're being attacked from all sides. I had heard of people squeezed up underground in the Great War, buried alive with their babies and having to be dug up, some crawling out days later covered in mud and missing their limbs and their little ones. I could see even Mama and Daddy were scared to death. I could tell they were glad I was the only one of their children left at home. If they lost me, there would at least be two left. I could see them thinking that.

Minrose and Stewart's house, rooted as it was on the Colonel's firm foundation, was one of the few structures left whole. (I always heard it was the *only* house left standing, but that, like many such stories, proved an exaggeration.) Much else had simply blown away. So the stronger-than-a-tornado house was turned over to the wounded and displaced. My mother said there were people sleeping in rows on the floors of all the rooms, like sprays in a funeral arrangement except that in their troubled sleep they would thrash about and cry out. The doctors stretched a man out on the dining room table to remove a tree branch that had blown through the calf of his leg from the force of the wind and come out on the other side.

They couldn't get it out, so finally they just gave him some whiskey to drink and cut off the leg after he had passed out.

A decade later, my mother would sit me on her lap and tell me about the little baby girl who was blown away. She'd belonged to some country people out from town and had somehow or other just flown right out of her mother's arms. They found her a day later, a little pink naked thing, tucked into a crepe myrtle bush. I imagine they didn't find her at first because the crepe myrtle would have been blooming to beat the band those pink fluffs that smelled and looked like moldy dust, and she must have seemed like a pretty clump of blossoms. They must have laid her on the kitchen table when they brought her in, and someone, probably Minrose, whose baby girl she was not but who had had two sweet girl babies, surely tucked her little arms over her chest and covered her with something, perhaps a clean blue and white checked dishtowel.

Then she must have looked like bread rising.

After my father left us high and dry, I also lived, with my, by that time, grown-up mother, who had survived pony fall, Great Tornado, and first husband, in the house at Church and Walnut, which was by then covered in English ivy and honeysuckle. My grandparents remained and so did relatives, front porch, fallen figs and lascivious wasps. Sometimes, in fact, what I think I know about my mother's childhood is actually something from my own: Alice Anderson's crashing chords (though she was blinder than ever and blundered at them), fogged iced tea glasses on the front porch (though the talk had turned to topics like the threat of Communism and the horrors of the Bataan Death March), the friendly mosquito fog (though in my time children were instructed not to run behind the truck because the spray might make us dizzy).

My early childhood—how can I say it?—was like the second draft of a story or the pentimento effect of a painting painted on an old canvas over an earlier picture. It had a resonance; it was something that had happened before but had yet to happen: history but also possibility. In those days my hopeful childhood, my delight in living as we did (it never occurred to me to miss my father, who, never spoken of, seemed to have vanished without a trace, except, of course, the trace of the little girl who looked, I discovered years later, exactly like him), must have seemed like an affront to my mother, now sad for her curly-haired freckled aviation cadet who had flown away, seeing me in her own place as daughter, herself straddling the worlds of daughter and mother, but not wife, not lover.

In my mother's things there is a snapshot cut in half. What remains of it is a picture of her in her early twenties. The scissors must have curved around her body like a delicious hand. She stands there looking directly into the camera, laughing as if someone had just told a joke. There is something on the left side of her waist. A shadow, but of what? A hand? An elbow?

My grandparents were polite people who at night read aloud and indiscriminately from *Evangeline,* the *Christian Observer,* the *Saturday Evening Post,* and, for my benefit, a host of *Uncle Wiggily* books. Around nine o'clock they would wish each other a pleasant rest and retire to their separate bedrooms. There was a door between their rooms, in front of which my grandmother kept her sturdy oak bedside table with a lamp and magazines and novels piled high. Someone, I don't remember who, told me that Minrose found Stewart a restless sleeper who kept her awake with his goings on.

I would wake up hearing my grandfather wander. He'd go into his study and read, or he'd go downstairs and drink a glass of buttermilk—you'd see the clabbered glass in the sink the next morning crusted with the previous night's buttermilk and cornbread. Sometimes he'd spend a long time in the bathroom. Or I would hear the front door open and close and the porch swing begin to squeak. I might wake to him sitting on my bed, patting down the covers (even on hot nights I kept the sheet over me, not wanting to be too surprised) and singing under his breath, "In the sweet by-and-by, we shall meet on that beautiful shore." His naturally raggedy voice would sound teary, as if he were sad about the sweet by-and-by and wasn't sure where the beautiful shore was.

Sometimes in the afternoons when my grandmother got home from school, she couldn't stop teaching. She would grab me up and make me conjugate Latin verbs with her. She'd get in her own rocking chair, which had thick comfortable slats of horizontal boards, and thrust me down in my grandfather's with its thin vertical slats, one cracked and protruding, that poked you in the back. She'd love to get me to rock back and forth with her and sing *amo, amas, amat, amamus, amatis, amant* over and over until we'd both get out of breath and start laughing. Me laughing and almost crying from that backstabbing chair of his. Then she'd tell me stories about ancient Greece and Rome and the people who lived and breathed larger than life in those olden days. Years later, when I visited the British Museum and saw the giant marble figures of wild centaurs and goddesses with cantaloupe breasts and great muscled horses struggling in battle, I knew why her eyes shone, why she, with her silver pompadour wave and skin that hung like a soft net over her bones, loved them so.

Sometimes in the middle of the night when I had a feeling about things, I would crawl into bed with my grandmother. I had once seen a picture of little brown bats pleated up with their feet curled under them sleeping on the side of a cave, and that's the way I would see me and my grandmother. The bed-springs were weary and I didn't weigh much, so after a while I'd roll downhill into the soft place of her back and stick there, like she was the cave. I still sleep with my feet folded together.

My grandfather had a temper, the Clayton temper it was called in the family. It would begin with a red face and went through various stages of apoplectic rage usually ending in something being thrown, though not with intent to harm. I felt the brunt of it early on when I stole one of his chocolate bars, which he stashed in his underwear drawer. As a girl roaming the big house alone I spent much of my time peering into other people's drawers and closets looking for things that surprised and transported me, like pretty handkerchiefs and fruited hats and old books with pictures of naked men and women, the lat-ter with open mouths and long dark hair, doing acrobats with each other. Once I found a small bottle of whiskey behind my grandfather's law books in his study, and later found another in the back of the medicine closet in the bathroom. Eva Lee Miller, who was always telling me she about killed herself tak-ing care of me — a statement that turned out to have been partly true when she died two decades later at age fifty-eight from a blood clot traveling to her brain after embarking on its jour-ney from an ulcerated leg (too much standing on your feet, the doctors said) — called me "Little Miss Nosy." (Eva, I later learned, kept my grandfather supplied with whiskey from the local bootlegger.) My mother, emancipated by Eva's presence in the house, had become the local Welcome Wagon Lady, and

I delighted in pilfering her baskets. She would come home from her rounds enraged by my thefts. Here she'd be sitting down with total strangers, which was the point of the thing, and say something like, "And here's a lovely potholder from Woolworths," and reach in to find it missing. I especially liked the spice samples from Nesbitt's Grocery and would hide them in my drawers to make my clothes smell like China.

When he couldn't find his candy bar, Pop Pop, as I called him, crashed around the upstairs of the house, slamming drawers and hurling the contents to the floor as he looked for the bar which I had eaten several days before. I crouched on the sofa downstairs crying and stoutly denying that I was the culprit. My mother stood over me with arms folded. "Little girls who tell stories feel guilty the rest of their lives," she said. "The-Holy-Ghost-hates-a-liar." (At the time the feeling was mutual. I couldn't stand the idea of the Holy Ghost. I would dream that he was chasing me all over the house; preachers always said the Holy Ghost wasn't a he or a she but a loving spirit, but I saw him as an old man with a tobacco-stained beard and a face the color and consistency of paste. In my dreams he'd be singing "Onward Christian Soldiers" and trying to smother me under the covers.) Mama looked at me hard and said that telling the truth was the most important thing in the world. Then she got out the hairbrush.

It is *hard* to tell the truth, I sobbed. I don't remember the truth, I said. I *hate* the Holy Ghost, I said.

Some stories are like stolen glimpses over the shoulder. What you see are only tracks down a darkening path. Erin Taylor's college notes are meticulous, her grades mediocre. She is a regular girl. She goes to the University of Mississippi, called "Ole

Miss." (A peaceful and safe place for such a girl, twenty years before James Meredith will enter The Grove, with its grassy knolls and bent oaks, the heart of a campus where brown women in white uniforms decades later will still cover lunch tables with spotless linen cloths before football games. It is here that James Meredith will be greeted by gunfire and the red-faced governor with balding head. But this is before that time, and Erin Taylor joins a sorority.) She lives in Barnard Hall. Her room number is 436R. At the end of the long spring afternoons, she climbs the steps slowly. There are wet half moons under her arms, and her calves are hard. She has notebooks with football players on the front. In her senior year, 1942–43, with Europe on fire and millions of Jews in the camps or mass graves and Americans who look like the enemy locked up too but on this side of the ocean, Erin Taylor takes courses in the Old Testament, Public Opinion, Minority (singular), and Voice. In Public Opinion, she begins her course by listing (but not answering) the following survey questions:

1. How many children do you want in your family after you get married?
0—1—2—3—4—5—6—over 6

2. How many children (including yourself) did your parents have? (Do not include dead children under one year.)
1—2—3—4—5—6—7—8

On March 18, she acquires this information in her class called "Minority":

Segregation—people apt to rationalize by saying it is a way of keeping peace between groups. Segr. is not new—prac-

ticed in Rome. Refs. in Bible. Russia, Poland segr. Jews in
Ghettos.

2 types of segr. — 1. Forced   2. Voluntary

All big cities have segr. — usually voluntary — Harlem,
China Town, etc. Negro segr. in every society.

Negro segr. by various laws in South. Laws are really
in order to preserve our dominance. Force negroes to pay
equal prices on buses, etc., but don't give them equal service.
Laws say theoretically that whites may not enter negro area
& *also* that whites may not enter negro section — same is true
of Indians — whites move in & take over but negroes & Indians can't.

But is Erin Taylor paying attention on this March 18? In
the margins of her notebook she is writing the name of my father over and over, along with the titles of popular songs like
"Black Magic," "As Time Goes By," "Where Was I?" There is
a half-smile on her face as she writes. I can see it. I have seen it
many times when I look out over the faces of those I teach.

"Miss Clayton, do you have a question?" I want to ask. "Do
you want to add something before we go on?"

And she will jump, guiltily, and say, "No."

Despite such lapses, Erin Taylor will soon graduate from
Ole Miss with a triple major in music, history, and social studies. And be grateful.

May 23, 1943

Dearest Daddy,

Daddy, I have never said very much about it but I do appreciate my college education and the effort you have put forth
to send me. I believe that the things I have learned, both
from books and from people, will stay with me all of my life.

Your "Baby" loves you very much and appreciates what you have done for her—

Lots of Love,
Erin Taylor

Sometime after college Erin Taylor stopped dreaming and married my father, the dashing young aviation cadet two years her junior, the "Al" whose brevity had fit perfectly in the narrow margins of her notebook, who got her pregnant with me, stuck around until I was born, though it's not exactly clear what kind of sticking that required, since he was still in the service and traveling from base to base. It was a June wedding, the unlucky thirteenth. My news clip is torn and frayed; the year is missing. I do read that Miss Alice from next door played the organ, I hope not gloomily, and that the bride wore ivory satin and carried a bouquet of gardenias centered with a purple orchid. But it wasn't too long before dashing Al dashed off, or so I was told, to live another life, never to be seen again by either of us. (I do not know whether he is now dead or alive.)

When I was nearly six, another flying man came to pilot my mother and me away. He had been in the navy. What he did particularly well was land night fighter bombers in a split second on aircraft carriers. "In a split second," my mother would repeat and her eyes would glow. He was blond with clear blue eyes you could see straight through. He always brought me a pack of Juicy Fruit. People said he looked like Alan Ladd but thinner. When I was in my early teens, my friends would get crushes on him. He didn't say much, but when he did, his voice was hoarse as if from disuse. One night, before they married in Minrose and Stewart's living room with my mother in a pink dress, since it was her second time (of course she called it "dusty pink," and it did look like that shade of crepe myrtle), I went to sleep in my grandfather's velvet chair and dreamed this man's face above the mantle. Slowly it turned into a skull, and I woke up to see the last of it flickering away in the fire's glow. It was in front of that same mantle, decorated in fall foliage, that they married. My mother wore a brown hat and the pink dress with rhinestone buttons, which she kept hanging in plastic in her closet the rest of her life. After the honeymoon to New York City, where she got lost in Bloomingdale's and hours later her new husband found her sobbing next to an escalator, Mama packed her bags and mine. My life in the cool dark spacious house of my grandparents, who sighed when my mother whipped me, was over.

The blue-eyed bomber pilot transmogrified into a silent traveling salesman who liked his biscuits flat and his cornbread crisp (if there were any light or fluffy part in the middle of his cornbread or biscuits, he would cut it out and place it accusingly on the edge of his plate) and who was always having us run to the bank to deposit money to cover checks written too soon. Erin Taylor ended up with three children, myself by the dashing cadet (later, I heard, turned gynecologist), and two others by the bomber pilot turned silent salesman—a boy, and then another girl whom my mother subjected to frequent tests for mental retardation and finally shipped off to a strict Episcopalian school down in the Delta.

In her teen years, my sister ran away from home often, as did my brother. Sometimes they would end up with me, and later my husband and daughter, wherever we lived, appearing on the doorstep looking frayed. Once, as my sister was making her escape, driving off hastily in the rain, the salesman jumped on the hood of the car, grabbing the wipers and holding on, his furious wet face glaring at her from the windshield as she jerked and swerved the car to dislodge him, which she eventually succeeded in doing. Finally she disappeared for a while to live with her boyfriend until everyone came to the conclusion she was forever lost. Then she let them know where she was: in an apartment across town.

Later in life Mama returned to college to get her degree in social work. She helped start the first home for battered and neglected children in our town, named "Faith Haven," and worked there until, for some reason I never understood, she abruptly stopped. I am also uncertain of the nature of the work itself. She told me she had "a real job" with a salary, and she went to work every day, keeping strict hours, but a letter thanking her for her extraordinary volunteer work is among her dusty papers. What she seemed to do well was to keep angry fathers at bay, or so she said. She told me she once stood in the door and would not let a man with a gun come inside to take his little girl home. No one witnessed this incident. Her bravery pleased her, she said, because it reminded her of her own great-grandmother (the Jane Stuart of the South Carolina wagon train) who during the Civil War stood in the door of the old place outside of town, a knife wrapped in her lace handkerchief, and wouldn't let the Yankees inside to capture her wounded husband.

Without a job and seemingly unable to get another one (her resume of the period reads, somewhat wistfully: "*Objective:* A responsible position, preferably in the field of social work, offering growth opportunities and challenge"), Erin Taylor, by this time in her fifties, returned to college a second time to learn to write poetry. Why this happened, I do not know. What I do know is that it happened suddenly. My mother fell in love with the dictionary. She began carrying notebooks everywhere and chewing thoughtfully on the tips of pens. Poems started appearing in the mail, tucked shyly into her letters to me, like pressed flowers. In her last decade she produced about sixty poems, many of which were published in small journals and anthologies. Six years before her death she decided to leave the salesman. It was at that point that she found out she had ovarian cancer, which had by then spread throughout her abdominal cavity. The site of my beginning had become the beginning of her end. Her symptoms—fatigue, gastric distress, diarrhea, bloating—and her age—early sixties—were classic for advanced ovarian cancer, but the doctor who had previously treated her for an irritable bowel told her to take Maalox because he, like most other people including me, thought she was imagining things. "My stomach is getting *huge*," she told me one August afternoon sitting in my car after a ride in the country. "I can't button my pants. I feel pregnant. And so tired."

She returned to the salesman when it became clear that she was going to have to fight for her life. After a five-year struggle with cancer, she died in the back of the ambulance a few days before Halloween in 1988. At her funeral, the Presbyterian preacher seemed to be saying that her life had meaning because it taught others how *not* to live; surely, I kept thinking throughout the service, this cannot be what he means to say. Erin Taylor's newspaper obituary mentioned nothing of her published poetry. Her tombstone, ordered by the salesman, bears the inscription "Beloved Wife and Mother."

These facts explain nothing. My mother was crazy. My mother went crazy. I'm not sure which of these statements is true; perhaps both are. During most of her adult life, Erin Taylor was considered eccentric and difficult to get along with by people who knew her well and people who had known her in passing. By the time she had gotten crazier and begun to do things like walk up and down the street in her bathrobe with stockings drooping and blooming at her ankles, she had become a town legend. But even as a child I could see people shrink from her and float away. Sometimes, in a church foyer or doctor's office or at the market, I saw their eyes flash in anger for something I knew she had done to them in the past. She was known for her temper, for the way she had of lashing out at ill-fated clerks, meter maids, her children. With a scarf wrapped around her pin-curled head, she cooked for us dry tasteless food and, every day of the week except Sunday, dusted, mopped, and scrubbed the small dark places in which we lived as the salesman added us like an odd assortment of toiletries to his travels through the world. While she fed us and cleansed our environment, she would scream at us and hit us with vigor and determination, as if this were part of her job. Most of her life she was very thin.

Later in life Mama became too sad (today we'd say she was chronically depressed, and that mental illness is not a crime) in the process of what most of us would see as a normal course of life events: her own mother's gentle decline into senility, the sale of the stronger-than-a-tornado house to the people with the red pot, and, finally, her mother's death. (Today we would give Erin Taylor her Prozac, which she'd probably flush down the toilet or save up to try to kill herself with, unsuccessfully as usual.) It was during this period that she stole the flowers off the altar of the First Presbyterian Church ("steal" is perhaps too strong a word because she was convinced, somehow, that they were hers to take) and, on the way to the cemetery to place the flowers on her mother's grave, which apparently was why she took them in the first place, ran a four-way stop, crashing into a young family of four (who were coming home from that same church). It was quite a scene, I was told, bloody screaming children and gladiolus all over the place, my mother not paying any mind at all to the children but gathering the flowers out of the street as fast as she could for fear someone would take them away from her or run over them. Fortunately, no one was seriously hurt and the damage was minimal, but not minimal enough for the insurance company, which had gotten increasingly disturbed over Mama's propensity to run off the road for no apparent reason and which found the four-way-stop incident the last straw and canceled her policy. "I had a little accident yesterday," she wrote me. "I just didn't see that stop sign. I think they put it up recently."

Then came the gyre: the anorexia, the overdoses, the constant battles with pharmacies, the flanks of roads looking better and better, lovely seductions at every turn. It all whirled inward, never reaching any conclusion. Once when my brother found her unconscious on the kitchen floor from an overdose of sleeping pills and she had to have her stomach pumped, Mama agreed to see a psychiatrist. After two visits she refused to return, saying she felt much better, thank you very much, and please mind your own business. The psychiatrist, a realist, gave me the gloomy report: "Your mother would have to be re-raised, and I don't think she's going to cooperate." At the time, and since, I've thought about that strange and awkward term "re-raised." If a student of mine wrote such a word, I'd furrow my brow and, if I had the energy, try to think of something to put in the margins to replace it.

In the final five years of her life, fighting the cancer with two abdominal surgeries and almost two years of brutal chemotherapy, Erin Taylor went over the edge. I committed her twice to mental institutions, the first time to a nice private one where southern women of a certain class were allowed to go to have respectable short-lived nervous breakdowns, and the second to Whitfield, the state hospital for seriously crazy people who will be staying a while (their relatives hope), especially those whose luck and money have run out. (When I was growing up, everyone was always talking about sending people to Whitfield; one did not go to Whitfield on one's own, it seemed—one was always sent. "They're going to send you down to Whitfield if you don't quit acting like a fool," Eva used to tell me. "He better watch out. He's going to get sent to Whitfield," it was whispered about my paregoric-loving great-uncle, Vann Jr. "Send them to Whitfield!" would be the affectionate joke about teenagers who acted silly and crazy at the same time the way teenagers do, but who would, everyone knew, turn out all right in the end.)

The first time I committed her, my mother tried to stab me with a pair of scissors. Fortunately they were dull, and she pathetically weak, weighing, in fact, less than eighty pounds, having eaten for the past two months only green beans. The second time, less than a year later, I got two deputies to go into the house. They broke through the front door and then the door to her bedroom, where she had locked herself in for the past few days. She was living on the floor of the closet, eating fig preserves and bread and butter sweet pickles with silver cocktail forks off of good china. She had stacked up all the phone books in the house on the closet floor, as if to keep herself company with all the people she knew, and whose names she had marked in red.

The way we knew she was in there and alive and kicking was the fact that she was singing at the top of her lungs. We could hear it through the window. "I hear you calling me, lovely Vienna, so gay, so free" and some arias I didn't know. My mother was always talking about Great Music, though the only opera she ever took me to was a bad production of *Madame Butterfly* that miraculously toured our town. (I was disgusted by the plastic cherry blossoms, which fell like stones instead of drifting down, as even I, a child, knew they should do.) She herself had a soprano voice that took your breath away and had been much in demand at weddings. At her high school commencement she sang "I Heard the Voice of Jesus Say," and for her college glee club Christmas concert, "And the Angel Said."

After the second commitment I drove six hundred miles to visit her at Whitfield. She came into the visiting room barefooted, took one look at me, snatched up the books and bedroom slippers I had brought her, and pronounced, "Minrose. You are the *last* person I want to see on the face of the earth." Then she put the slippers on her feet, threw the box and boxtop at me, turned, and stalked out of the room. I sat down on the plastic-covered couch and stared at the wall, waiting for her to come back, but she never did. That was the last time I saw her.

After my mother died, I began to have dreams.

I am walking through a maze of dark hallways. I turn a corner; in a shadow my mother is standing there dressed in black. Her clothes, and she, seem to be unraveling, coming to pieces like shredded bits of tissue, layer from layer. She does not speak; she will not let me pass. We are both frozen in place, but she is coming to pieces and I can feel myself turning to stone.

Or I open the door to my closet and find her on the floor, her feet tucked under her, leaning like a monk over a stack of telephone books, turning the pages with fingernails long from death growth, writing names on a pad. I lean down to see who is on her list, and her unexpectedly strong hands, so like mine, and her mother's before her and my daughter's after me, pull and pull until I am lost to her greedy arms.

Once at the university where I taught I had to change my office because I dreamed that my dead mother stood in the door with arms and legs astride and trapped me inside. The flatness, the banal look of her grave site with its easy mow-over style of tombstone, when I finally visited it several years ago was odd to me, for it seemed that her power, the sheer force of her, should make the ground hump and crack over where she lay.

When my stepfather remarried, happily, joyously, at almost eighty years of age and then died several years later after being lovingly cared for by his new wife and his children, he was not buried in the plot reserved for him beside my mother. In an obituary, she was not mentioned. My brother began to worry about Mama being alone in her grave. He decided he ought to move her, place her next to other family members to make her feel less lonely. I began to have nightmares about her popping up in outrage at the disruption, hair flying and lipstick smeared, looking like she looked during her commitment proceedings or when discovered on the closet floor in the dark.

Once, as a fledgling newspaper reporter right out of college, I covered a disinterment. Maybe because it was Mobile, Alabama, a general bogginess of the cemetery grounds, Spanish moss everywhere, an early morning drizzle, that bringing up the coffin seemed so, well, sad. Sad and unclean. Later my brother wrote that he had changed his mind. He did not say why.

Today, my mother's birthday, I am sitting in my backyard in the Rio Grande Valley of New Mexico. I am following my mother's tracks. The loamy ground beneath my feet was, a millennium ago, under water. I sit reading at the folding card table my mother gave me when I married, hastily, in 1969. "A card table comes in handy," she said. And it has. I wrote my dissertation on this card table, stacking it high with heavy library books. I threw a bedspread over it for my daughter to play by herself in a basement apartment in which nobody could ever be alone. When the flower children of my generation were taking off their clothes at Haight and Ashbury and singing about peace, I listened on the radio and tie-dyed shirts for myself and my daughter out of cooking pots I had put atop my table. I stacked a hundred boxes of Girl Scout cookies on it when I was block captain and studying for my comprehensive exams. I tried and failed to learn to sew on it. At one point I cut it with a sharp tool, how or why I don't remember, and now it has a long, deep slice that runs diagonally across the top. I have covered this wound with thick electrical tape, which, as the years have gone along, wrinkles and dries and must be removed and replaced. When I left my husband of nineteen years and moved to New Mexico, I almost didn't put the table on the moving van. At the last minute, the woman whom I left my husband for said, "Let's take it. You never know when you can use a card table" (which she indeed has used each spring to start her seeds early). So on the truck it went.

Today this table is loaded with old papers, scrapbooks, letters, clippings, documents, cards, pictures. These were found and sent to me only recently. Some are from almost a century ago. I work here in the backyard because they are so very old, and I am violently allergic to them. Inside, they make me sick. I can read them only when I am out in the fresh air. In the past few afternoons, when the rains come in, the winds come up in unexpected gusts. If I am not careful to place rocks on my piles, everything will blow away.

What these papers from my pack rat mother tell me is that the truth is even harder to tell than I thought. That there was an *Erin* who existed in a world apart, who inspired passionate correspondences on literature and art, who was cherished and admired by people I never knew or even heard her speak of.

From a ninety-three-year-old Jewish man from Northport, New York, a recipe for Hebrew Cookies and a request: He wants to know *everything*—yes, *everything*—about his dear friend Erin the poet who has become dearer and dearer to him as the letters have flown back and forth between them. Anything she says will be poetry to him.

From a grand-niece, who was then twelve: "Dear E.T., I agree with you on Bach. He and Handel are my favorites. . . . You must always remember I love you. A lot of people love you. You are so sweet."

From a younger man, who confesses in pages of impeccable, minuscule print that he is manic-depressive but is resisting lithium because he must have his wits about him in order to write the one perfect poem when it comes to him, which it surely will. There is a poem about to be born in him. Nothing has jelled yet, but the chaos from which order is created is there. And he will create. (In my mother's handwriting on the back of the envelope sent by the poet-in-waiting: "these silver-misted moods of summer rain").

Above my head, in the giant and lushy green sycamore with its bark peeling and dropping like tendrils from an immense reptile, is a hummingbird nest the size of an egg. In it, two tiny beaks point to the sky like the tips of a pair of scissors. The mother has become accustomed to me and no longer buzzes fretfully around my head on her way from flowers and feeder to nest. She is resigned to my presence at my table under her most precious of burdens. She does not worry that her babies, in their first efforts to fly, will fall kerplop into the dust of dead people's lives. She knows that she, and they, are unlike other birds. They will open their little wings, and they will fly without failing.

There is a belief that a person does not move into the realm of the dead until there is no longer anyone left on this earth to summon the lost one by name, to call her back to the lovely earth. Now, today, here in this place, I can call my mother's name. But one day, sooner rather than later, there will be no one.

And then, hearing only blessed silence, she will unfold her crowded heart, and depart.

III

Tuesday November 25, 1930

Dear Diary I am so eccited because Friday I am going to Columbis to see sister and I might take you with me.

Wednesday November 26, 1930

Ant Rose sent me a chokolite turkey today for Thanksgiving. I bit some off of it. But I am going to get a piece of paper and color it dark brown. And paste on the place I bit in on it.

Thursday November 27, 1930

Gee! I had a grand time at Nonawayne's party. It was a Thanksgiving party. This morning I went and gave some things to a poor criple little girl. We had turkey and everything to go with it at Nonawaynes party. The paper said it was going to snow. Daddy said he didn't think it would tho' I hope so I adore snow.

IV

LAST NIGHT I HEARD THE
CHILDREN

Last night I heard them
heard the children crying
and I saw them
        seared
scarred and cross-scarred
the lamb blemished
again and again.
The stars were veiled
and the earth was filled
with the sound
of weeping.

And I held them
all night long warmly
within my arms I held them
           inviolate
in the shelter of my dreams.

ERIN CLAYTON PITNER

My mother wrote this poem when she was grieving her own
mother's death. I want to part these words like hair and see
into my mother's face. Her face is the first thing I remember.

In that first moment—that pulp of mouth and eyes and voice—
I am conscious of the dense fact of the bars of my crib. I see
what I will later come to understand is the face of a woman. I
want that face. The bars run up and down between that aspira-
tion I will soon know as myself and the flesh that shines and
croons. I reach through and touch filament, which I now know
was hair, which I remember as dark.

Some stories make us see. Then, like selfish children, they
snatch seeing away.

In photographs taken when she was a girl, Erin Taylor
smiles gamely, a small, dark-haired girl with, even then, Miss
Erin's full mouth and round eyes. Her jaw tilts forward, as if
she is ready to kick off her shoes and climb that old mimosa
down on the street corner's edge, the one my cousin would
later climb up into one night to perch like an exotic bird whose
clipped wings had grown out just enough for the flight to the
branch but not to the sky beyond, who wouldn't come down
until there were threats of fire trucks and sirens waking the
neighbors.

In the few old snapshots I have of Erin Taylor as a young
woman with me, her sweet baby girl, she has one absent-
minded hand on me or an arm around my middle. Her other
hand hangs at her side. It seems misplaced, limp. Her eyes gaze
into the distance, not at the lens but at something else much
farther away. She looks squeezed between me and the now-
gnarly mimosa.

There are two vertical lines between my mother's eyebrows.
She is young, twenty-five at the most, and smiling. But still
they show.

❊ ❊ ❊

THE MIMOSA TREE

for the children, wherever they are

> Will the blossom return to the branch,
> or the broken mirror reflect again?
> —Buddhist proverb

Do you remember the first crimson cadence
of the cardinal in April
and frail blue mornings drizzling fragrance
after rain?
The mockingbird shrills your demise to heaven
decrying the jagged whine of the saw
shredding your body limb by limb.
Nothing left but roots cradling
broken pink blossoms.

Go back now. You were planted at dawn
and the children wait for you to unfurl
the slender green fronds of day.
The boy will notch the summers of your life,
every grievance gnarled to the tallest branch.
The little girl will become the mother coaxing
each child back to the square brick house
for baths and supper
in the fragrant hush of June darkness
drowsing about your feet.

It is enough. Stop there
with small faces, dream-tossed
at the doorway. Blossoms blown back
to the tree.

ERIN CLAYTON PITNER

Under my New Mexico sycamore with its spiky balls and unkempt nest (the hummingbird mother is too busy for house-keeping; she is exhausted by these ravenous twins), I am wishing for mimosa blossoms. I know they are nearby. It is July and I can sniff them out. Maybe later I will take a walk and pilfer a few from my neighbors' tree. I will put them in a jar on my card table, hold my hand over them when the afternoon winds come. I will twirl them under my nose as I work.

On my card table the strained white faces of boys and girls peer at me from the high school yearbook. It is my mother's class, the sophomores, arranged during the lunch hour, by their peckish teachers no doubt, like upright knives and forks at a haphazard buffet. The children are standing on the steps in front of the brick school building. Theirs are serious faces; their class motto is serious: "Knowledge comes, but wisdom lingers." There is much to be serious about. The year is 1937, and the stirrings in Europe are worrisome to these children's parents; soon they will become worrisome to the children as well.

I search the faces, once, twice, three times, for my girl mother. I cannot find her.

Did Erin Taylor miss the class picture-taking? Home sick with the sniffles, a fever, the measles, crying her eyes out because of her absence on this of all days? Is this the fault of that misbehaving pony? Or is she here, under my very nose? Is it possible that her face is indiscernible to me?

I look for her in other parts of the yearbook, which does not include individual pictures of the little sophomores. There is only space for girls selected as

Most Popular
Most Beautiful

Wittiest
"Personality Girl"
Most Versatile
Most Athletic
Most Intellectual
Best Dressed

Erin Taylor, called "Tatie" by her friends, is none of these.

When I was little and snooping into the backs of things at my grandparents' house, I found Tatie's high school diary in a closet. Each day's space was carefully filled with entry after entry of repetitive recitals of events. "Ate oatmeal for breakfast." "Did my homework." "Went to the twins' party." Superimposed again and again on top of the entries on every page in the year-long diary were the words "I LOVE L.M. I LOVE L.M. I LOVE L.M. I LOVE L.M." This passion, girlish though it be, surprises me. I never heard my mother say I LOVE, I LOVED this one or that one. The sneezy dust in these old boxes, she might say, is more to be trusted. (In a poetry notebook dated 1980, I read my mother's notes toward a poem: "Love is a turncoat, a switchblade at the throat." She will be approaching sixty when she comes to this conclusion, and it sounds irreversible.)

But then love was not the blade but the flower: the bud. Flamboyant scrawlings on the Greetings pages of Tatie's senior year scrapbook:

Dearest Tatie, I love you more than you will ever know. May you live long to do the things near your heart. Here's to all our little chats. Love & hugs, M.F.

Tatie, I'll always love you just as much as I do now. May your future be as happy as the present. Don't ever forget the one who gave your famous nickname. Love, J.

Tatie dearest: May your life be bright and sunny, and your husband fat and funny. Love B.

I used to imagine new lives for my Tatie of the loving girl-friends. I pictured her with cropped hair and flowing scarves around her neck, living an avant-garde life with Natalie Barney and her salon on the Left Bank in Paris. (My mother would say Paris, France, to distinguish it from Paris, Tennessee.) Or a thin novice on Sappho's island, a girl plucked from the country with a heart-stopping soprano voice. A girl who sang her very own poems to the pulse of waves and the murmurings of women.

Once, when she was in her late fifties, Mama got into a lesbian writers group by mistake. She answered an ad for a women's writing retreat in a rural upstate New York village called Oneonta. She was accepted and went up there for two weeks. I began to receive letters saying things like, "There are some *very unusual* people here."

When she got home, she whispered to me on the phone that she thought most of the women there were homos. I asked her how she could tell, and she paused. "It's the shoes," she said.

She liked the homos all right, she said, but she didn't think she'd tell anybody but me about them. She said she wrote more during those two weeks than in any other time in her life, though she felt a bit left out of things.

❋ ❋ ❋

In her high school days, Tatie kept, in addition to the diary, a scrapbook of clippings. On the first page is a picture of a beautiful woman cut from a magazine. Her skin is white and delicate. She is wearing a silvery suit with puff sleeves; a corsage of pink roses and daisies is pinned over her left breast. She is sitting in a floral upholstered chair and her head is turned in profile so that her gleaming marcelled waves show to advantage. Her lips, cheeks, and fingers are discreetly tipped in pink. She is a work of art. Everything about her seems motionless and precise. Under this picture, which covers most of the page, is a list, also cut from a magazine.

RESOLUTIONS

I will try to be popular at school this year
I will not be catty, jealous, or snobbish
I will try not to think of myself all the time
I will widen my interests so that I can talk to anyone
I will practice good manners—even on my family
I will make the most of what good looks I have

The clips that follow are poems with titles like "What Shall Be Left of Beauty When You Die?" "A Garden Path," "Song," "Woods Pool," "Sonnet to Autumn" (not Keats), and "Rain in the Country." There is a program for the class play, called *Lunatics at Large,* and a clipping of King Edward's Farewell to Britain.

In the middle of the poems and on the back of the page with the picture of the beautiful lady is a photograph of a girl in a tartan plaid skirt and white blouse. She is grinning broadly and holding onto a kitten with both hands as she poses for the picture. The girl's shirttail is coming loose, and you can tell that the kitten is about to wiggle out of her arms. The girl does not look like she will ever grow up to become the lady in the clipping on the other side of the page or, for that matter, someone for whom King Edward would give up the kingdom and the crown.

My mother's life should have been bright and sunny. She loved to sing and dance. In her later years when such things became affordable, she had a small portable radio that played scratchy love songs, and she carried it everywhere around the house, even into the bathroom with her. Until the cancer, her energy was boundless. In her late fifties, she wrote to tell me about her dance class: "We had more fun at dancing last night than I have almost ever had. She kept us overtime. We did ballet, of course, disco, cha cha, Wellington, the Stomp and the Charleston. Wow!"

In her later years she came to like what she called picnics, although that was not precisely what they were. The process that led to a picnic went like this:

MAMA: It's a nice day. Let's have a picnic.
THE SALESMAN (who was neither fat nor funny): [Silence]
MAMA: We don't have to go anywhere. We could have it right here in the backyard.
THE SALESMAN: [Silence]
MAMA: Or just the porch. Now the porch would be nice. I'll make some egg and olive sandwiches and we can sit right here on the porch. Just a little picnic . . .

Such conversations occurred only when someone else besides the two of them was present; otherwise there would be no one to have the picnic with. The salesman would not sit down and eat anywhere but at the table. If the picnic on the porch won the day, he would take his sandwich to the kitchen counter and eat it standing up.

EGG AND OLIVE SANDWICHES
(a picnic recipe from your mother)

1. Half dozen eggs, hard boiled—don't boil them too hard, but hard enough.
2. Some chopped olives—the green kind, stuffed, slice them thin so that the red pimento looks pretty.
3. Miracle Whip—not too much.
4. Mustard—put in a lot of this, almost as much mustard as salad dressing. You want a bite.

Mama liked bite in her food and put some combination of mustard, Worcestershire, and ketchup in almost everything. Minrose before her and Miss Erin before her had all their lives eaten good rich food prepared by other women who stood long hours over hot stoves and sat wearily alone at the kitchen table to eat their own midday dinners after clearing the white folks' plates, washing the saliva off their dishes, and sweeping up around the table. ("I'm going to tie a chicken to your chair to eat up all these crumbs," Eva would tell me, the little Minrose whom she did not get paid extra for looking after.) While having her solitary meal in the kitchen of the stronger-than-a-tornado house, Eva would read the paper, if she could get her hands on it. I would sit with her more often than not, but she did not like to be disturbed if she had the paper. After she ate, she would rise groaning on her massive legs and carefully cover some leftovers to take home for supper in the tin pie pan she brought to work every day. Eva stood at six feet two inches and in her prime weighed over two hundred pounds. She was always talking about her legs. They pained her, she said, even when she was sleeping; then she would dream about limping up to the Pearly Gates and hollering out: "Just lighten up my load, Saint Peter, and I'll know I've come to the right place."

After marrying the salesman and heading out for parts unknown, Erin Taylor had neither house nor cook. But Eva's careful steady ministrations had spoiled her, and as a consequence, she couldn't cook either. (Her mother, Minrose, excelled at chicken salad and tomato aspic, each of which had three ingredients and which she made triumphantly for her Saturday Matinee Club. Growing increasingly plump as she aged, indeed eating everything in sight the winter after her Stewart died in August, Minrose enjoyed thinking about food, driving Eva crazy about what she'd fix that week or next Sunday—"Look out, Lord Jesus," Eva would mutter under her breath, "here comes that eating woman again"—or spending half an hour at a time on the phone to Mr. Nesbitt down at the grocery store, asking him what the chuck roasts looked like and whether the raspberry sherbet had come in for the summer.)

In the early days of Erin Taylor's marriage to the salesman, when she was trying to get the cornbread flat and learn how to shell black-eyed peas, which turned her fingers purple, her favorite dish to prepare was corned beef hash. He told her to stay home, he would make the living, so she had plenty of time to think about the best way to prepare the hash. (When things got desperate she would run for the bus to go to temp jobs—"just until you get on your feet," she'd murmur to him, pulling us out of the bed before dawn when the phone call from the agency would shatter our quiet breathing, leaving the heart pounding through breakfast.) She would open the can of hash, grease a shallow Pyrex dish with bacon drippings she kept in a crusty jar on the top of the stove, and mush the canned hash down in the dish. She would bake it at high heat to brown it. About halfway through the browning, she'd ice the mushed-down hash with Heinz Ketchup.

"It has to be Heinz," she would say, "or the whole thing is ruined."

The corned beef hash days were traveling days. My step-father was a traveling man. Like the absent father of Tennessee Williams's imagination, he had fallen in love with long distance. During the six years after he married Erin Taylor with me tossed into what would prove a bad bargain all around, we moved so many times I lost count. One year I had grade school pictures from three schools. Some places we lived I never even got to school because I would get sudden onsets of mysterious combinations of sore throats, coughs, swollen glands, runny noses, headaches, earaches, and toothaches that sometimes lasted for months. We lived in two- and three-room apartments surrounded by concrete parking lots. Little houses behind regular houses. Loaned houses with odd-smelling furniture from relatives whose eyes always looked past mine to something over my shoulder.

Whenever the salesman (who was then the salesman-to-be, for he had not yet found his true calling) forfeited another job or ran out of rent money, we would head out for another place, usually around dusk, when the mothers in the apartments would be calling their children through lighted windows for supper and baths, the time of day a dear familiarity drifts through the coming dark. We ran into a wild boar on a dark road in Louisiana; I fell out of the backseat where I was sleeping and hit the floor with a thud that kicked the breath out of me. We were stranded until morning. We saw the bluebonnets in bloom in the oil fields of Texas, slapped our wheels in mud over long, straight roads across the Mississippi Delta. My brother was almost born in the backseat of the car as we tore across the city of Houston, Mama first moaning then hollering bloody murder, to get to a hospital, any hospital.

Today, on Central Avenue in Albuquerque, the famous old Route 66, I see a traveling woman striding down the street. A blanket is folded around her shoulders like resting wings. She looks like a praying mantis. Her hands are flapping high over her head, furiously gesturing in what appears to be sign language. This walking woman seems to be talking to herself, the one hand saying some brutally offensive thing and the other screaming back in rage. These two busy angry hands piece something together in the space between them, the space directly over the woman's head. I think the woman, who is thin, is hungry. She has lost something she is hungry for and is telling hungry stories to herself as she travels.

As we would move from pillar to post, I would think about my "real father." I knew that he sent fifty dollars a month, enough, I learned, to use me as a tax deduction so that the salesman could not. He was bound by law to pay for my college education. "Bound by law," I once overheard my grandfather the lawyer say to my mother. "I made sure of that." These were the terms of the divorce, and in those days they were considered very good terms indeed. At Christmas my father, aviation cadet turned doctor (later I would imagine myself going to him as a patient under an assumed name, just to see his face, though the fact that he was a gynecologist was sufficient deterrent), would send me one special present that cost more than all of our gifts put together: a topaz ring (my birthstone), a strand of pearls, a typewriter, a velvet dress, a charm bracelet with one charm: the physician's serpent whose coiled outline was raised in rough gold. My mother, her full lips pursed, would give me the latest present, which would always be beautifully wrapped from a department store.

I knew to take my special present into my room to open it. "So Nobody Feels Bad," my mother would say. When I shared a room with one or both of my siblings, I would take it into the closet to open it. Then I would put whatever it was away, and nothing more would be said about it. As the years went by, I acquired a stash of such fine things. They were like dirty magazines hidden in the back of my closet. The cards, which I threw away, would read, "Love, Daddy." Each one in a different handwriting.

Except for these gifts, which I came to dread and loathe, I have the cut-in-half photo and the scrawls in the margins of Erin Taylor's notebook to testify to my father's actual presence: absences that signify presence. (I also have, I suppose, myself as testament of his existence.) In the cut-in-two photograph, my mother's features, which had hardened by the time of the picture-taking with me as a worrisome baby in her reluctant arms, are more indistinct. She looks as if she is giggling at a private joke. She looks like she's having one hell of a good time.

I wonder what I would see had the picture remained whole: another young face—young enough to be my own son now—a face that would also harden, in anger perhaps, in sorrow, I would hope, to give up a beautiful wife and fine girl baby. My mother would not talk about it, but I know that at first it all happened like a dream come true. There was a wedding picture of her stowed away in a buffet at my grandparents' house. I used to take it out in secret and study it for hours. My dark-haired girlish mother, almost twenty-three, under the veil her face thrown open like a church door on Easter Sunday.

Fourteen months after my birth, the divorce was final. Someone, I don't remember who, once told me that it was my father who wanted out. My mother never spoke about him. My aunt said he was a happy-go-lucky guy who liked to tell jokes, and she gave me his ID tag from the war. After the divorce he'd sent it to her in the mail to give to me so that I'd have something with his name on it to remember him by. He was twenty-two when I was born, just too young, that's all, everyone said. A nice fellow, everyone said.

In my mother's papers, I find a short story entitled "A Journey." It is about a young woman named Ruth Ann. As the story opens, Ruth Ann at the close of the war has received a letter from her serviceman husband telling her he wants a divorce: they married too young, then there was the war. Now he wants to hike the Tetons and find out who he is.

Ruth Ann, who lives with her parents in Mississippi and has a year-old girl baby, packs her bags and a picture of her baby girl and hops a bus to New Hampshire, where her husband is stationed. She finds him in the Officers' Club having a good time; they have dinner and sex, but he is up early the next morning and leaves Ruth Ann lying in bed struggling to wake up and saying, "Wait, what about us?" She shows this less-than-enthusiastic husband and father her prize picture of the baby girl, whom he dutifully admires but does not inquire after. She returns home with the realization that he cares nothing for either her or the baby girl. This fictional husband and father is, as the schoolteacher Minrose would later pronounce my young father, "shiftless." Thus the marriage ends and the story ends.

On the last page of one of my mother's notebooks is a fragment of an unfinished poem, called "Ruth Ann":

> She would fight
> clear of it all—
> the cloying solicitude,
> the empty aphorism
> the hollow enunciation
> of love
>   clammy with insincerity
> as sure to fade as
> brief interlude of
> clematis playing in the
> August moonlight, ashen
> and shriveled at September dawn.

But of course the story goes on: The sweet girl baby and her mother are left behind in a land of dreamy summer nights. They are blossoms blown back to the tree.

The mother is sad. Will anyone rescue her from the stronger-than-a-tornado house? Will anyone save her from the fate of becoming a Welcome Wagon Lady with blue hair?

The navy pilot, soon to become the salesman, can land his plane on a dime. He is blond and handsome. Yes, he was in jail once for bouncing checks to pay off gambling debts, but that's then and this is now. He kisses the left-behind mother and she turns into a princess.

And off they go to see the world and have many adventures. But the sweet girl baby, who is now a girl, sometimes sweet sometimes not, follows reluctantly. She begs to be sent back to what was her home, but her mother will not give her up. Years later she will find in the dresser drawer of her dead grandmother a letter in large block letters without a signature:

DEAR MEMUM
I WANT YOU   COME GIT ME

Finding ourselves in a five-story concrete building in Houston, Texas, my mother and I become part of a group of women and children who get together in one of the apartments and exchange food every couple of weeks—some rice for some beans, some potatoes for a ham bone, and so forth, just to get through to payday. (Almost all the men in the massive multi-unit complex, including the salesman who is not yet a salesman, work for Brown and Root, which pays its less-than-adequate wages, or so they seem to us, twice a month.) Erin Taylor shells black-eyed peas and we have peas and thin cornbread, sometimes with milk, sometimes not. My mother's best friend is named Tommie, a bent-over Kentucky hill woman with a straight-line mouth who looks as if she has no blood in her face, she is so white and thin-skinned. Tommie, my mother will say, "has more children than she can handle," and I can tell that my mother is afraid of becoming Tommie, though she loves her only friend—I can see that she loves her—and tries to help her out with bits of things, a bag of flour here, a few onions there.

Instead of cooking, since there isn't much to cook, Erin Taylor spends hours ironing linen napkins and cloths for the table, a card table, an older version of mine, which she sets up in the living area for each meal. She always lays out a salad fork and teaspoon, even though we don't have salad or dessert. After the meal, she holds them up to the light, examines them for crumbs, blows on them and puts them back in the drawer. I, meanwhile, am dreaming of Sunday dinner at my grandparents' house. Pork roasts, legs of lamb, rice and gravy, butter beans, fig preserves spill off my plate in my ravenous dreams. One night I awaken to find a cockroach sitting in a pool of saliva next to my mouth.

One day some older boys, some of them Tommie's boys I think, chase me around with the bloody tails of puppies their father has chopped off the day before and thrown in the garbage. The next day a stray cat mews and rubs my leg. I pick it up by the tail and whip it around my head in a circle and slam it into a concrete wall that separates our apartment from the road. The cat screams like a woman, falls to the ground, scrambles over the wall. There are honks and the squealing of tires. I put my hands over my ears and run screaming into the apartment.

Another time it floods, covering the tops of cars. Water moccasins take up residence on the stoop to our apartment. My stepfather has to sweep them off with a broom before he can go outside.

Now we are in Victoria, Texas; my mother has fallen into a huge crack in the ground when she is out hanging clothes. Her foot is broken, and I must take care of my little brother, who cries all the time because he has boils under his diapers.

In Jackson, Mississippi, my second-grade teacher, until she is later fired, is stealing her students' meal tickets and taking each of us out in the hall in alphabetical order for whippings with a large wooden spoon. Why she does any of this we do not know. We sit bent over in our desks, afraid to look up. Before the teacher, whose name is Miss B., is found out and fired, my mother sends me on a trip with her to visit my grandparents about two hundred miles away. Miss B. has discovered that she and I have relatives in the same place and tells my mother she is driving up to see hers. She won't mind if I come along, for the company. I am scared to go but it is the only way to get back home.

En route Miss B. will not take me to a rest stop or service station to use the bathroom. She makes me urinate on the side of the road beside the car. She makes me leave my door open and watches me squat awkwardly on the pavement. She keeps one hand on my thigh the whole trip, moving it only to shift gears. I am afraid to breathe. She drives past the turn off the highway to my grandparents' street and will not stop to let me out.

"There it is!" I jump up in my seat and point to the street by the gas station and the drive-in diner. "There's the turn! Right there at the light. *There!*"

She pushes the gas pedal down.

"You missed it! Just drop me off right here then, Miss B. On the side of the road. I can walk. That's fine too."

She looks at me as if she can't remember what I'm doing in the car with her, as if she is seeing me for the first time that day.

"I'm late," she says. "I want to see my people too, you know. I'll bring you back later on."

She takes me to see her relatives, who live on a dirt road on the outskirts of the county, and makes me sit on the front steps of their trailer for hours. I sit there with all the chickens pecking around me in the dirt. I watch the sun crawl across the afternoon sky. A little girl with a runny nose brings me out a glass of water. Finally, when the sun is gone and there's only a bit of pink left, Miss B. comes out of the trailer and tells me to get back into the car, that she's taking me back to town. She drives me back to my grandparents' house, stops her car under the big oak tree at the curb, takes off her wide black patent leather belt, and hands it to me without saying a word. Then she puts me out at the curb with my suitcase and drives off before my furious, shaken grandparents can burst out of the front door.

I used to take out the belt and look at it. It looked wounded at one of the holes where she had worn it too tight. Once, in a fiction workshop, I wrote a story about Miss B. and the trip. I made myself into a boy. The professor said the story did not work because nothing really happened in it and there wasn't enough dialogue.

Because we move so often, my mother quickly learns to take typing jobs that are temporary. She goes from being a Welcome Wagon Lady to a Kelly Girl. She is popular with the Kelly Girl people because she can type and file. Now we know that the phone will ring early in the morning, so we set the alarm. Then we will not have to scramble for her to make the bus. Now if the phone does not ring, the two lines between my mother's eyebrows look freshly plowed. When I get older, she will make me take typing in high school. "If you can type sixty words a minute, you can always support yourself," she will say with a shake of the finger, and I will believe her because I have the evidence. (My first real job in high school, not counting working at my uncle's drugstore, will be to type the city tax roll on a manual typewriter with a carriage the length of a base-ball bat, but much heavier. One summer for eight hours a day five days a week, I will sit in a small hot room and type the whole tax roll onto ledger sheets. *Smack,* will go the carriage over and over, and at the end of each day I will go home and put a heating pad on my left shoulder. At the end of the sum-mer, the left side of my upper body, including my breast, will be noticeably larger than the other and there will be a slump to my shoulders. I will beg to be allowed to find a job as a wait-ress, but my mother will say waiting tables is not a nice job for a girl and can lead to trouble.)

Broke and jobless ("Daddy simply cannot work for other people," my mother told me), my stepfather moves us back to our hometown when I am eleven. As he becomes more and more silent, my mother screams louder and longer, as if trying to force him to speech. He is not easily forced. He has the eyes of a hawk and nerves of steel. He is the oldest of five boys who were beaten regularly by an alcoholic father. (They lived on a big farm place out from town, and he was always trying to hide his brothers, my mother told me when I was older; he would stash them around the place like half-chewed bones, silent tow-headed boys in closets and chicken coops, on the floor of the old pickup, just to get them out of sight. This father one day went to the doctor's office, walked into an examining room, lay down on the table, practical man that he was, and shot himself dead. In the chest, my mother said.) The salesman can drive out a tank of gas in a car without stopping. And then get an-other tank and move on. I do not think he likes the sound of the human voice. He is gone more and more. He speaks so little that when he does speak, we all stop what we are doing to listen.

Yes   No
Erin Taylor quit it

His words carry a power that can change our lives in a breath, without warning or pause. (Years later I am involved in committee meetings at a university where I am teaching. One man on the committee never speaks. After the rest of us talk about this and that, the difficulties of and different approaches to a specific problem, exhausting ourselves in the process, the department chairman always says, "Well, 'Joe,' what do *you* think?" At that point "Joe" tells us what he thinks and then the department chairman does what Joe says to do.)

I am lying in my bed. On the other side of the paper wall, there is a woman screaming at her husband: *If it wasn't for you and your big you-know-what, I wouldn't be in the shape I'm in. I hate you hate you hate you.*

I hear him laugh deep in his throat.

That summer my sister is born.

Now the salesman is a salesman. He is on the road from Sunday night until Thursday or Friday. "In business for himself," my mother says with a little click of her teeth when asked what her husband does. There is no money, barely enough to feed us; we are loud pulsating young bodies in small rooms of tight places. We bounce off walls. We fill up and overflow. When he is on the road, Erin Taylor screams at us, we cry, she whips

us—everything seems jagged. When he comes home on the
weekend, we have to be quiet. We are actively quiet. We buzz,
we whisper in corners. (Looking back, I know from the way
he'd fall on the sofa that he was dead tired, that he had worked
hard, that all he wanted was peace and quiet. He would turn
his face to the back of the sofa and I would look at the lines on
the back of his neck. They looked like highways crossing and
recrossing.) When a friend calls me after nine, he explodes
from the sofa and, without saying a word, jerks the phone out
of the wall while I am whispering into the receiver. When he
is home we have better meals, but we have to wait for him to
speak at the table. There is no music, no silliness in our house.
We struggle for goodness.

Once when my mother goes out to run some errands and
instructs me to watch my brother and sister, I tie my brother
to the sofa with a rope so he will stop running around the
house. I trick him into thinking it is a game, but then I won't
untie him. He cries and cries but at least he is not running all
around trying to get hurt while my sister is crying in her crib.
It is too much, the two of them together.

*Selfish   selfish   all you are is selfish   I work work work all you do
is whine and cry   Minrose take them outside   Get them out of the
house   out of my sight*

At mealtime Erin Taylor slams the plates down. She is getting thinner. The more arduous the meal preparation, the worse
she is at the table. The slightest gesture triggers a slap, a
scream. Once I try to fry chicken for her. This, I am told, will
earn me a Girl Scout cooking badge in addition, I hope, to
pleasing my mother, giving her a break. I burn the chicken and
myself and am covered in greasy splatters. Sit down, I tell my
mother, try to get some rest. Tonight the supper is *my* job,

tonight you can relax. I feel dizzy by the time I sit down to eat my meal. Nothing comes out right. The chicken is raw inside. You have made a terrible mess, she says in a voice like broken glass.

After a while she begins to make smaller and smaller meals. We become sitting vultures at table, ready to snatch whatever's sitting still. My sister quakes and stutters when she eats, always spilling something. My brother, who seems to be shrinking rather than getting taller, drinks gallons and gallons of milk and still becomes anemic. I visit my girlfriends at mealtimes. My sister becomes thinner and quieter. Her head hangs down like a bell.

The salesman is now joining organizations that call for Accuracy in this or Law and Order in that. "This is good for him," my mother will say, to no one in particular. He goes to meetings on how to get rid of Communists and restore Our Way of Life. He starts getting mail from the John Birch Society. My mother keeps his supper hot on the stove. She screams at me when I take the lid off his plate and try to pick the bottom crust off of his cornbread.

As I approach puberty, my mother becomes obsessed with my bowels. She is deathly afraid that I will not pass my bodily wastes. Every morning I go into the bathroom and pretend to defecate. She sends me to the doctor for imagined hemorrhoids. Yes, I tell him, I go to the bathroom regularly. No, there is no pain. No bleeding. Not any. Do you have a boy friend yet, he asks.

One night, when my daughter was about three years old, I hit her over the head (I would point out that I choose my verb carefully; I wanted to use a saucy one like "bop" but it wasn't a bop; it was, I'm afraid, a hit) with a purse I had just wrestled away from her to take to a symphony concert I could ill afford but had been looking forward to for weeks. Those were the days when purses and shoes were supposed to match, and I was pleased that mine did. It was a brown patent leather purse that matched my brown patent leather shoes. She didn't want to give it up as a toy. It was empty and small (notice how I excuse this act) but I was immediately horrified at myself. I had become my mother. I was hitting my daughter with handy objects around the head and face. How could I do such a thing? My daughter was shrieking. My husband was shocked. I burst into tears and ran from the basement apartment, convinced that I was not fit to be a mother, that the demon that had possessed my mother now had me in its clutches. I was doomed. My child was doomed.

Listening to the music that night, I embarrassed myself, as I often do, by crying in public. The movements of the music kept splashing back onto one another, dredging bottom. I was thinking that it is a delusion to imagine ourselves beyond the opus that marks the very curve of our bones. Flesh and heart fold back. Always.

That night after I got in from the concert, I sat for a long time in the dark by my daughter's bed. Then I went into the kitchen and got a flashlight. As my daughter slept, I shined the light on her head, parted her hair, and looked for scratches and blood. I found a red spot. Would it become a bruise? Would it swell? Would it be noticed? I smoothed her hair back down and put my hand in front of her mouth to make sure she was breathing, the way I had done when she was a baby. I sat beside her until dawn. The streetlight outside our apartment made her face white like marble.

When you get home from school this afternoon   you're going to get the worst spanking you've ever had   young lady   with the hair brush   with the bristles

About once a week when I was little I would do something and my mother would call me upstairs to her room in Minrose and Stewart's house. I would climb the long gleaming wood stairs, the light from the upper windows shining in my face. I was not supposed to cry out loud but sometimes I did. When I would come out after a while, Eva's lips, which were thin anyhow from her Choctaw grandmother, would be in a pencil line, and my grandmother would be pushing hard on the front porch swing and kicking her plump stockinged legs together. My grandfather would have left the house.

During the day, Eva told me not to pay any attention to Mama, life was not easy, take one day at a time, try not to aggravate my mother, stay in the kitchen out of people's way. Did I see *her* complaining? Eva let me help her cook and made doll clothes and lace bonnets for my doll. I walked her home in the afternoons and she and I would sit around drinking iced tea in her Jim Walter shell home with the unfinished insides and hanging sheets for doors, even to the bathroom. I used to help Eva feed in the material while she sewed at her machine since she had no little girls or boys of her own to do it and her husband Hiram worked days and sometimes nights too. One summer we made all of the band uniforms for Carver High School, which had a large and jivey band that jumped and hopped its way down our street to football games. We saved the scraps and Eva made me military-style doll clothes with gold braid and brass buttons on blue serge.

Sometimes Eva would take one long hard look at me and

say she was sick and tired of little white girls messing with her stuff, enough was enough, and she would send me home.

At night my grandfather would read to me. I would sit next to him on the sofa in the cool dark living room, the chosen book in his lap. I would turn the pages. We read all the Uncle Wiggily books. The old gentleman rabbit had a bad case of rheumatism, but armed with his trusty crutch and valise, he knew how to get around, traveling in the most splendid and hazardous ways. He flew in airships that took him from one adventure to the next; he got stuck in mud holes; he fought off alligators from a paper boat; he cured Grandfather Goosey Gander's epizootic with a cup of catnip tea; he was saved by a colony of courageous ants from a bad giant who wanted to eat him for dinner but ended up having baked beans instead.

Uncle Wiggily gave me a lust for travel. In dark closets I secretly packed my grandmother's handbags and pretended they were my traveling valises. I would get my grandfather's cane and tote it and my bulging valises to the top of the mimosa tree on the corner. I would twirl the mimosa blossoms against my nose and smell the sweetness of cherry blossoms in Asia Minor. I believed I was mounting the skies in my own airship, ready, like the old gentleman rabbit, to find my fortune and look for adventure and danger.

Danger is not always where you think it will be. During the last stage of my mother's craziness, about six months after I committed her the second time, a large shelf fell on my head as I was photocopying class materials at the university where I was teaching. The shelf was loaded with debris, cleaner fluid for the copying machine, reams of paper. It had partly pulled out of the wall once and now chose to fall on me, the buzzing, harried flesh below leaning over the machine, arm extended holding down the book, copying, oh dear, last minute, an essay for class. I was knocked to the floor, my head twisted to one side like a half-broken tree limb. My neck was wounded, both obviously (tingling, numbness, a whiplash) and mysteriously (searing and chronic pain, but nothing discernable on the x-rays).

As part of many treatments over a period of years, I agreed to try hypnosis. The first time the therapist tried to lead me into a hypnotic state, I began to envision myself going down the steep stairs into the dark cellar in my grandparents' house; the tornado is coming and I am going to be blown away. My mother, her arm in a cast, is crouching in the dark where the stairs turn. She is telling me to hurry up, come on, the storm is coming. She pulls a long pointed object out of the cast, but I cannot tell what it is. (In actuality, I don't remember much about this cellar except that the old black furnace thumped along down there and there were stacks of old magazines. I used to peer down the long flight of wooden steps into the hot noisy darkness below. I do not remember ever venturing down.)

As the therapist (assumably) droned on, I began to sob. I felt as if I were choking. Hastily she brought me back to reality. The next time we try it I find myself going *up* the stairs in my grandparents' house. Now I feel myself drawn by a blinding light. As I ascend the stairs, I begin to whimper, then sob, but I cannot stop climbing. I glide up toward the light. I am small again; the steps seem high to my feet and legs. I am afraid, but I cannot stop climbing because someone upstairs is calling my name. Up and up I go, sobbing, whispering *no no.*

Then the therapist pulled me back, and I found myself soaking wet with my own sweat. I felt as if I had been snatched from a burning building, or a grave.

"No more of this," I say.

"Maybe not," she says and scratches down some notes.

In those before-the-salesman days, Erin Taylor loved to sing, and she always sang as loud as she could. Later this would become a source of much embarrassment to me, and to my brother and sister when they got old enough to be embarrassed, which was very early for all of us. Although the First Presbyterian Church had several hundred members, you could always tell when Mama was in attendance. She sang the doxology like the Apocalypse was right around the corner, and as if she were having a hard time convincing herself that all blessings flowed from God the Father. She had no sense of decorum or blending in. She sang as loud at funerals as she did on Christmas and Easter. Around the house she sang her favorite again and again:

> *I hear you calling me,*
> *lovely Vienna, so gay, so free.*
> *City of love and sparkling wine,*
> *you're such a part of this heart of mine.*
> *I hear you calling me,*
> *echoing out of the used-to-be . . .*

As she pushed her cart along grocery store aisles, she would sing

> *Somewhere over the rainbow*
> *bluebirds fly.*

Birds fly over the rainbow.
Why, then, oh why can't I?

When she sang, it was as if she were pushing something too large through her throat and mouth, sound that was more than sound, that was somehow being forced into voice, and by being forced, became beautiful.

Shhhhhh, we would say. Mama hush.

YANG OR YIN

for Sylvia Plath

Speak so

ach   ich

skein of words bitten off
at the quick.

Not this

ooh   aah

legato of lips
diffident as the dawning of she
who first gazed at the earth awe-struck.

Click consonants between teeth
crisp as pebbles
learning their Greek.

Disdain the vague flutter of natal hands
upon your face
or the tremolo of nestlings
at evensong.

Wring words.
Pare to bone.
Twist neck of swan
until her blood run black
and her eyes pop dull as stone.

ERIN CLAYTON PITNER

In the end all I wanted was to shut my mother up, lock my mother up.

My cousin Lynn and I are sitting in a tiny windowless room in the county courthouse with the court-appointed lawyer who is rubbing his plump face with a dirty handkerchief and asking me questions. Lynn is my second cousin who is my age and whose mother, the southern belle younger sister of the first Minrose, used to let me stay part of the summers at their house in Virginia. We all knew it was to get me away from my mother but no one ever said so. (My brother and sister would look angry when I left; their faces would be closed by the time I returned.) When her parents would take me on vacations with them, Lynn and I would sit under the boardwalk at Ocean City and comb each other's hair as the waves came in.

As I try to answer the lawyer, I suddenly hear my mother's voice. Unbelievably, she has escaped from the deputies and is coming down the corridor. I hear her long before I see her. *"You can't stop me. I want to see my daughter the one who did this to me. Minrose! Minrose! Where are you? You'll pay for this, young lady."*

I begin to tremble. Suddenly she rounds the corner and appears before me framed in the open doorway, dyed black hair plastered to her head, her clothes hanging off her withered frame, red lipstick looping snakelike over much of the bottom half of her face, her stockings fallen to her ankles over filthy bedroom slippers.

She lunges for me. Her hands are claws going for my eyes. The lawyer sits there dumbfounded, handkerchief in midair. My cousin, who is now a therapist and less afraid of crazy people, jumps between my mother and me and shouts for attendants to come get her.

I am told that my mother, as the person being committed, has the right to be at her own hearing. In principle this seems only fair.

In court she screams at me during most of the proceedings in which various witnesses and the court psychiatrist speak in hushed tones of her lunacy. I feel humiliated for her and, as always, mortified by her behavior. I want to shut her up.

She asks the judge, a former classmate of hers, how he can possibly think of putting her in a mental institution when they used to go out together in high school. Red-faced at this disclosure, he sternly tells her she's sick and he is going to send her where she will be taken care of. It's for her own good.

When they drag her out of the courtroom screaming at the top of her lungs, stockings unraveling down the backs of her ankles, I feel as if someone has taken a brick off the top of my head. When several weeks later she falls out of her bed at the state hospital, probably, I now realize, from oversedation, and breaks her hip—*breaks her hip*—I am *glad* because that means they can't discharge her anytime soon (the first hospital had kept her a grand total of seven weeks, which I suppose is the time allowed for respectable nervous breakdowns to run their course).

Sept. 4, 1987

Dear Mama,
I'm so sorry to hear you have broken your hip and wish you a fast recovery. I've been keeping up with you through your doctors, and I want you to know I care for you very much.
Love, Minrose

So what I did was this: I locked up the woman who gave me birth and I was glad of it. I have no excuse. I might well do it again. Be wary of me. I'm not a person you'd want around if you went crazy.

Several years ago: I am in a meeting of a feminist journal editorial board. We are considering a short story for our journal about a daughter visiting her mother in a nursing home. One woman in the collective says: "I would never put my mother in a nursing home. My mother died of cancer last year and I took her into my own home and nursed her through it until she died. I couldn't stand the thought of anyone else doing it. I nursed her like she was my own baby. Like she was my own child."

She looks at the rest of us expecting some sign of approval. Instead we look at her blankly. We are middle-aged women with old mothers or dead mothers.

I feel my mouth fill up, suddenly and unaccountably, as it would when I was first pregnant.

Everyone said I did the right thing. The salesman had packed up, or pretended to, leaving a letter to me stating that Mama was indeed on the closet floor and there was nothing to eat in the house and he was sick and tired of everything being in an uproar (he later reappeared when I got her safely contained).

My brother in his twenties left home and started growing. Six feet and still counting. How tall is tall enough? My sister the youngest, her brother and I flown the coop (she spent much of her childhood hiding somewhere, sometimes the closet): well dadgumit if she *wants* to stay in the closet. . . .

Neighbors and relatives calling. Something must be done. It's *your* mother. But the truth is I did what I did for me as much as for her.

I suspect my motives.

In class we are reading "The Yellow Wallpaper." One student asks: But *why* does the husband want to lock his wife up? I open my mouth to answer. The terms "patriarchal power" and "the confinement of women" roll off my tongue. I talk biography, the history of "the rest cure," Freud and Dora and hysteria. The masculinist bias of psychoanalysis.

I am thinking (how can I admit this?): Maybe it was more than he could take. Maybe he felt he had no choice. Maybe she was dangerous. Maybe she hurt the baby.

"Maybe we need more clues," I say.

My Clues (what I still have):
A Comfort Inn note pad:

> —get blue gown in top of chest
> —paranoid psychosis
> —antisocial behavior
> —personality disorder
> —get bourbon for myself
> —suicide attempts—3 that we know of
> —fetishes—cuts up material and stuffs it in her clothes, dishes and food stashed in closet and under bed, etc., etc., will eat only green beans

—longterm facility or 24-hr nursing care
—$$$?

The back of an envelope:

—CT scan
—atrophy of anterior cerebral cortex
—senility poss.
—Alzheimer's??? No
—rapid deterioration
—violent
—starving herself
—dangerous
—knives everywhere

Is Erin Taylor still angry that I locked her up? As I write, I begin to feel that she has somehow, like a shiny fish, slipped through the net that separates the living and the dead. She has slid, not unexpectedly, into this room where I sit at the computer. I am getting so that I come in here only to feel her glide through my eager fingers (which, yes, Mother, are fast at the keyboard) before I can sink the bait and catch her for good. Before I started writing this book yet again (I've written it many times in the past dozen or so years), I liked this room, its cross breezes, its pictures of my grandparents and my daughter, my grandfather's velvet chair I used to nap in when I was little, the view out back of my grandmother's iris, which have traveled with me over a dozen or so moves in five states and, like those who travel and plant at the same time, remain, in part, where they have been.

The iris were originally yellow, salmon, purple, and lavender. They used to be planted in huge beds, covering sections of my grandparents' backyard. Old-fashioned single-shade iris. Over the various moves, I have lost colors without knowing it. I would always dig up most of them but I always wanted to leave a few where I had lived. I wanted them to be like the iris or jonquils you see on the side or median of an interstate sometimes. There's no house left, no people. But you know that some sweet-faced country woman lived there once, and she had her yard and flowers. She would work in her flowers around dusk, still with her apron on, when all her other work was done. As dark drifted, she would kneel in the dirt, a wisp of graying hair slipping down over her solemn face.

But it is tricky to move iris rhizomes. They mutate underground; if you move them when they are not blooming (and they shouldn't be moved when they are), you do not know what colors you are taking. So you can end up with more or less than you think. At one house that bordered on East Tennessee woods, I left my salmon iris without realizing it in the fall. In Virginia, when I left my husband in the dead of January, I dug up most of them but somehow lost the dark, dark purple ones, my favorites. Now I have only yellow and lavender left. I miss my pretty others, but there is no getting them back.

You talk flowers   I had more beautiful flowers than you ever thought about having   clematis like sweet cream pouring over the trellis out back

My mother has stretched out on the bed I keep in here for company. She has no intention of leaving. She has a thin cotton blanket covering her feet just to the ankles. Her head rests on her stained blue satin pillowcase. She has on a barely visible hairnet so she won't mess up her hair with this little rest. One arm is thrown over her eyes to block the light. It's two o'clock, her time for a nap.

By four she'll be up and galloping through the house, ready for the company she always expected to come but who seldom did, or for a trip to the A&P, where they'll politely put her bounced checks in an envelope and mail them back to her. At midnight she'll still be up, maybe cleaning the stove or taking a bath singing under her breath some sweet sad song of love.

In the morning she'll wake me singing about how lovely Vienna is calling her and bumping the door to my room with the vacuum cleaner. She'll holler through the door that I'm lazy and to get up right this minute. Or she'll have to come in and get me.

How to explain it? How to mark the moment? The day the wheel turned and Erin Taylor slipped away.

Dear Minrose, why am I writing today? Because it is raining again and is totally dismal—a cold November rain. (I can't get out to walk.) Do you remember the day it snowed on your birthday? I had taken you children to the movie and planned to go to the drugstore but had to take you slipping and sliding all the way.

Love,
Mama

Was Mama *always* this way, I used to ask my aunt, my grandmother. (By the time I was asking this question, there was the slope to my shoulders from the city tax roll, my hair was chopped, and I was jumping out the bedroom window after sleep overtook my weary parents, who slept in the dining room of the little house we were living in at the time, pushing off the salesman's old green Ford and taking rides in my shorty pajamas, a Lucky Strike hanging from my lips, at one and two in the morning. I would pick up my girlfriends and we would find boys and drag-race. We almost witnessed a murder at the local bootlegger, backing up when the face-down body came up in the headlights and the bootlegger himself jumped out of the bushes and said, "Get the hell out of here." On summer nights we parked on dirt roads in the middle of nowhere to drink out of warm cans as the boys would lean into our open car windows. I was fourteen.)

In response to my question, my aunt and grandmother would shake their heads gravely and murmur, well, not exactly, but there was always something strange about Erin Taylor from the very beginning. "*You* know how your mother is," my grandmother would say. Then she would stop talking and look out over the elephant-ear leaves of the fig tree outside the window and rock back and forth in her rocking chair.

I would look at her solemnly, facing her straight on and rocking in my grandfather's backstabbing chair, which had, unaccountably, become even more painful to sit in during the year after his death. I did not want to let my grandmother out of my stern line of vision. I would wait it out for her to say something more. We would be so close our knees would sometimes touch as we rocked. I'd be thinking *amo, amas, amat,* as I always do when I sit down in a rocking chair and rock. After a while she would pat my knee firmly and begin to talk about something else.

When I was twenty-one they discovered that my mother had a goiter. It was removed, and everyone breathed a sigh of relief: *Thyroid. That's* what caused the rages, the nervousness, the moods, we said. But she was just the same. Her eyes didn't bulge as much. That was the only difference.

Wait.

Erin Taylor is waking up from her nap on the bed in my office. She is telling me she's sick of the sound of my voice. Shut up and listen.

All that talk and you don't know the first thing about it. I was in my prime. All you children. Long nights and the smell of the mimosa. Dog-tired all the time and when he'd finally come home after being on the road all week he'd never even talk to me. Just threw himself down like a stone. If he'd just said something to me how's the weather been here or how's your mother or what have you been up to all week it might have been all right.

CRAWL SPACE

for a young poet

Bury your light beneath
a bushel of corn pone and white turnip
to warm the cockles of his heart
lest you find yourself alone
at table.

Sleep small in the hidey hole
you fashioned for your own
unless you've outgrown it.

And when you've stretched every nerve
and fibre of your being, trim the poem
without flinching.

Fling the gauntlet, pay the piper,
dance while you may.
Dwell in hell or a pumpkin shell
for time enough and space
to be.

ERIN CLAYTON PITNER

My mother's fleshy words slide in and out under my fingertips. I think it would surprise the Erin in my office if I told her she is dead.

Like Miss Erin before her, Erin Taylor didn't take surprising news well. In 1969, when pregnancy prompted me to marry (or at least so it felt in a time of back country "chiropractors" whose sidelines were coat hanger abortions), I did not tell my mother. I called her long distance and told her only that I had gotten married at the courthouse in Knoxville, Tennessee. She was startled and furious. It was not that she didn't want me to marry. What she wanted was an engagement picture in the paper and parties. She wanted me to wear the long dress and have the wedding in the First Presbyterian Church. She wanted to *sing* at my wedding. She had her heart set on it.

She tried to get me to have another "real" wedding and pretend it was the only one. I said no. As the months passed, I did not go home. I did not tell her I was pregnant. Every morning after my shower I would look at my naked self in a full-length mirror, deeply shocked at the loosening of tissue over the sinister thickness below.

The baby was due in November, around Thanksgiving. When I finally told Mama I was pregnant, it was September. I dieted strenuously and told her the baby was due in early January, which would have been nine months from the date on the marriage certificate. She was horrified even at that piece of (false) information. She then told everyone that the baby wasn't due until February. I guess she was hoping it would be late. (Now all this seems the height of absurdity, a comedy of errors.)

During my pregnancy, I smoked, drank, and dieted. I held onto the baby until almost Christmas, at which time the doctor, who was afraid I'd spoil his holiday, induced labor—much to my consternation—after I had come in with a bit of cramping that had stopped. (Left to my own devices, I believe I could have held on into the new year.) Five minutes before my daughter was born, I sat up on the labor room table, crossed my legs, and informed the nurse that I was absolutely not ready to have this baby.

From all reports (*I* certainly didn't call her), my mother was outraged when she heard that she was the grandmother of a seven-pound, eleven-ounce healthy girl who was obviously not premature. I brought my baby home from the hospital on Christmas Eve. It was snowing and the snow was so wet that it stuck to the trees like cotton in the fields.

The Junior League ladies had made bright red stockings with white satin trim and bells on the toes for the Christmas babies. When I carried my daughter into the house and laid her on the bed, her face was as red as the stocking she was in. I looked down at her and realized suddenly I knew nothing about being a mother. I had been so busy trying not to have her, I had not even thought about what to do with her once she arrived. On the big bed, in the stocking, she looked wrong, as if she'd been left there by somebody who didn't want her or blown away from her real home. I was afraid to touch her for fear I would hurt her. My husband hurried out and bought a Dr. Spock book.

All Christmas Eve night and into Christmas Day I waited for my mother to call me. She did not. When twilight fell early that night, I began to cry. I cried for about the next twenty-four hours without stopping. Everyone said it was postpartum blues. My husband sat with me for hours while I cried; then his mother took over. Then he called some of my friends to come by. I told everyone all the sad things that had happened in my entire life. Nobody could get me to stop crying. Finally the baby started wailing and wouldn't stop either, so then there were two of us boo-hooing and finally I had to stop so that she would.

After several weeks passed, Mama relented and took a Greyhound bus to come see the baby, but when I carried her out to place in her arms, she refused to touch her. She was sitting in my rocking chair and when I tried to hand my perfect child into my mother's lap, she crossed her arms over her chest and refused to take her from me, all the while rocking back and forth as hard as she could. The next morning she went back home.

Soon afterward I got the Hong Kong flu and ran fever of 105 over a period of days. I had been breast-feeding; my mother-in-law had expressed her skepticism about this form of feeding by purchasing a baby scale and weighing my daughter before and after each feeding to ascertain whether, in fact, she were receiving nourishment and, if so, how much. When my fever spiked, my doctor said over the phone (no need to come in, he said; everyone has it) to keep the baby away. He did not tell me what to do with my overflowing milk. My breasts became so engorged that, in the emergency room I ended up in, when the doctor put the frigid stethoscope to my burning chest, I screamed in pain.

He was not a native speaker and he did not understand what was wrong.

"What?" he said, alarmed.

"Ow! Breasts!" I said.

"What? Something with chest?" he said.

"*Breasts HURT!*" I screamed. "Nursing!"

"What nursing?" he said.

"*Baby! Nursing Baby!*"

I did not hear from my mother for several months. Then one day a package arrived with handmade baby clothes in it, exquisite little white dresses with tiny embroidered buttonholes and roses and daisies on the collars and pockets. The seams were hand sewn. My mother had gotten a woman to make the dresses. They were for a newborn, delivered, I guess, at the time my baby should have been. My daughter had already outgrown them but I kept them in the same box they came in. I have tied the box with yarn and moved it whenever I moved. Once my daughter found them and wanted to use them for doll clothes but I would not let her have them. Sometimes I take them out of the box and smooth them out and lay them on the bed all in a line. They look like flowers blooming.

❋ ❋ ❋

Packing my mother's things after I committed her the first time to a mental institution, I found the dozens of pages of text she had hand copied in the closet from a book I had written several years before. I could barely make out some scrawled phrases about struggle and the price women sometimes pay for lives they do not necessarily choose, words that, as I write them now, sound less complicated than one would wish. At the time I thought how sad, how peculiar: Erin Taylor has copied my words, taken my words and put them down by hand. I think now that she was taking back what was hers, the treasure of her life I had filched in the night and melted down into something both recognizable and strange.

Last letter from my mother postmarked September 13, 1988: Scratches on paper. One sentence of medicated chicken scratches on a dirty torn envelope.

Dear Minrose,
I wanted to be free like you are but I just can't get past that writer's block.

> Lots of love,
> Mama

In the last days of her life, I was not on Erin Taylor's mind. After the shelf fell on my head, I was immobile most of the spring, summer, and fall of 1988. Two scans showed nothing, but the pain was beyond belief. I would lie on my side and look through the slats of my window to the foothills of the Blue Ridge in the distance, and I would feel my mother's absence like fog over the mountains.

Now, after her death and the salesman's a decade later, her papers piled around me in cardboard boxes swollen with mold and the occasional embedded roach, I find my letters and cards to her in her final months. They are sealed; that is to say, they were never opened.

Or so it seems. I have tried to persuade myself that they were opened carefully and then were resealed by moisture in their imprecise vaults.

I open them, for the first or second time I do not know.

Aug. 22, 1988

Dear Mother, I'm sorry to hear you've been having trouble with your stomach and hope that you're better. I hope you got the potted plant. I had an accident several months ago which resulted in a severe neck injury. I'm flat on my back or in traction most of the time. I'm on disability leave this fall semester. I wish I could come see you, but I can't travel. I can't even sit up very long. I'm sure I'll be better eventually, but it will take time and patience.

I am sending the pressed clematis because I know how much you love it. Do you remember sending me a pressed clematis from your vine? They are beautiful this year — more beautiful than I ever remember.

Love, Minrose

Hallmark card with sunflower.

Sept. 1, 1988

WITH THOUGHTS OF YOU

May knowing
that you're thought about

Right this very minute
Help to
brighten up your day
And put some sunshine
in it!

Mama—Hope you're feeling better. I'm still an invalid myself
with this neck injury. Please know I love you and think about
you every day even though I can't come down.

Love, Minrose

Hallmark card with wheelbarrow and garden.

1988 (month and day illegible)

TO BRIGHTEN YOUR DAY

If knowing others think of you
Can brighten up your day,
Then surely these few lines should bring
A bit of cheer your way—
Because they're sent with all the warmth
A greeting can express
To tell you that you're thought of
Far more often than you guess!

Dear Mama, I think of you every day and wish I could see
you. I'm seeing some gradual improvement in my neck but
it's slow.

I'm sending you some of the fall leaves from my yard.
I wish you could see the yellow birches, red maples and
oaks, purple plum and dogwood, and yellow tulip poplar.

I'm worried you're not getting the stuff I send. Please
fill in the note and send to me.

Love, Minrose

These cards and letters of mine are an embarrassment, I
now realize. Vapid and weak hearted. Troubling the waters of
my own pain. Better left unopened, to be sure. Why, then, did
my mother keep them? Maybe she thought she would change
her mind and one day tear them open, a starving woman on a
desert island who keeps back one box of crackers and one day
rips open the box and snatches them out in giant handfuls.
Maybe she wanted me to find them, a decade later, in these
moldy boxes and measure the long flight of her absence, and
mine.

On my card table I set my letters aside to read the letters
and cards from these months that Erin did open. These are
true-hearted letters from pure-hearted friends. They are not
from wicked daughters who locked her up in a dungeon and
weren't sorry when she broke her hip. I imagine her holding
these true letters to her bloated belly after reading them again
and again.

From one of her men poet friends: "Good morning, Erin.
The way I read the situation, you are gaining strength — in
mind, body, and spirit. . . ."

From a woman poet: "I count you as a dear friend, and I'm
pulling for you with all my heart. Don't give up." (Erin wrote
"Keep" on the envelope of this one.)

And another: "I keep you in mind and hold your hand along
the way — Can you feel it?"

And yet another, the old man from New York again: "I

think of you a great deal; and I would gladly take your pain on my shoulders."

In the cardboard boxes I also find bits of paper and envelopes torn into scraps. These are pieces of letters my mother never mailed. One such remnant seems to thank my sister for the fall mums I actually sent.

Another is in an envelope, never mailed, addressed to herself. Inside it reads: "Dear Erin, the yellow bells are blooming at home and I'm very homesick but hope to be home—I'll try to call you when I get home, but if I don't, you call me."

Several other pieces are requests or demands, addressed to no one, or perhaps, anyone:

"Come get"
"Can't stamp"
"Need pencil and paper"
"Toothbrush"

In one, the signature: "Lots of Erin."

A friend says that once, when she was little, her mother was driving her around in a car and they were forced to stop quickly. Her mother threw out her arm to keep her from going through the windshield. "That's the one time I really felt my mother's presence," she says, "the only time."

I remember that my grandmother's hands smelled of glycerin and rose water and chalk. I remember hugging Eva's tree-trunk legs with their bandages and running sores and her rough, mostly friendly hand on my head. I know my grandfather's bones were sharp at the pelvis.

I do not remember my mother's arms around me or her touch on my face. I do not remember her own true smell or the texture of her flesh. Whether this is a failure of memory or of imagination, I do not know.

Dear Erin,
I am trying to get in touch with the one who wrote the poems. Please forward this letter to her wherever she is.

Love,
Her Daughter

V

Monday December 1, 1930

I have come back from Columbus and I sure did have
a good time. I thought I would die last night I was so
lonsome. I bought so many nice things. I have such a
bad uslsir I don't know how you spell uslsir, but I can't
help it. Jane Stuart wanted me to take some old milky
looking stuff. I hope I will be better tomorrow. Goodbye
until tomorrow.

Tuesday December 2, 1930

Well I took some Milk of Magnisn. Jane Sturt put a lot
of water in it. But still it was terrible tasteing. My uslsir is
horrible looking. It is white and real red all around it. I've
got to go to bed know.

Wednesday December 3, 1930

I think mother is going to get me the teddy bear I want
for Christmas. I think she told somebody in Mongumery
Wards to put it up until Christmas. Because she acted
sorta funny whenever I mentenied it. Good bye until
tomorrow.

VI

Dear Minrose,
I don't know where she is. Sometimes she was here and sometimes
she went away.

Your Mother

P.S. I do NOT approve of homos.

When I left home to go to college fifty miles away, my mother
wrote me long letters usually twice a week. They were full of
news—who had come by to see her, her latest class or job, a
copy of the church bulletin, a careful account of the health of
various family members and friends. She would instruct me to
write her back. She would send me stamped note cards with
directions to write Cousin Somebody or a friend of the family
who was ill or who had a loved one die. I read her letters casu-
ally and threw them away. There were so many of them, and
they became tedious to read, with their long discussions of the
weather at home, as if I were a thousand miles away, or her
visits to my grandmother in the nursing home. I did not keep a
single one.

After she was committed for the first time, I had not even
gotten back home to Virginia before a letter from Erin Taylor
appeared in my mailbox demanding that I come that very

minute and get her out of the mental hospital, even though she had to admit it was a nice one, and restful too.

Following her second commitment (admittedly an odd word for locking someone up against her will) she wrote me outraged notes of one or two sentences scratched on the outside of empty sealed envelopes. The mail carrier was beginning to look warily in the direction of the house when he dropped off the mail. The salesman had put me on every right-wing mailing list imaginable, so I was getting mail from the John Birch Society, Accuracy in Academia and/or Media—I can't remember which—the National Rifle Association, this and that conservative think tank, and many more. At the same time, mailings with pictures of bloody baby sea lions and appeals for southern legal defense funds and oppressed women everywhere were arriving. Mother's scratched-up envelopes with the writing on the outside for all the world to see were inserted into this already schizophrenic mix.

why did you lock me up in this horrible place
you are the most ungrateful of all my children
get me out of here this minute minrose or you'll pay for this
under court order like a common criminal in a police car

when i get out im coming to get you
youll be sorry sorry you did this to me
you think youre so smart dont you
well you have no   heart

One day two pink envelopes arrived, bearing the identical message in slightly different wording:

Dear Minrose,
I wish you would change name to Rosemary, for you do not have the
right to call yourself by Mother's name, for you are the most ungrate-
ful person I've ever seen in my life and almost regret that ever bore
you. By the way Dr. Woff and has said that may be able in 4 or 5
weeks.

Mama

Dear Minrose,
I wish you would change your name to Rosemary, for you have
betrayed me so badly by sending me to Whitfield that you should
not bear the name of Minrose.

Mama

My husband, weary of it all but especially weary of the bar-
rages of missives from the nuthouse, began to destroy the envelope messages before I could see them. By then, I was having
trouble breathing at various intervals in the day and was crying
when I wasn't gasping for breath. Sometimes I did both at
once. ("Are you having trouble breathing in or out?" asked the
doctor. "In," I said. "Then it's not asthma; it's *anxiety*," he pronounced triumphantly, writing on a pad of paper a prescription for Valium and the name of a therapist.)

It was mid-August. I had just gotten back from the second
commitment proceedings and was preparing to plunge into
preparations for the fall semester's teaching. I was immensely
relieved to be doing everyday things, putting a calendar with its
steady one-two-three march before me and mapping out, in a
comfortably predictable way, the readings for my classes. I was
therefore surprised to find myself crying in the shower at

home, then in the bathroom at the university library, and soon in more conspicuous places like the grocery store.

When I burst into tears while doing sit-ups in my exercise class to the tune of "All you need is love," I became coldly afraid. I knew I had gone over a ledge. I had not locked up the craziness; I had brought it home.

Then I got an envelope with this message:

Dear Minrose,
I wanted to be free like you are but I just can't get past that writer's block.

Lots of love,
Mama

It is true that you go over a ledge. That is, you walk out to the edge of the drop, though at the time you're thinking you're on solid ground; it's difficult going but you will make it, no problem. Suddenly you look down and realize you have taken yourself too far. You have gone past anything you could have held onto. Everything has fallen away and there is only the vacant-lidded blue sky. It all happened when you weren't noticing where your feet were. You are in a free fall.

This happens every few years to a less-than-cautious nature enthusiast who drives up the winding road to the crest of the Sandia Mountains east of Albuquerque. It occurs most often on one of those fall days when the sun is too bright, when, at eight thousand feet, the evergreens give way and you begin to see the yellow aspens with their quaking leaves, a joyous sight indeed. It is truly a splendid day, and you might be thinking that, though weary and overburdened, you are, remarkably, still in the luminous moment, present and accounted for in the world of leaf and branch and sky. The crest trail has many ledges that lure the traveler out, for the panorama of being on the top of the world, for the sense of flight at ten thousand feet, for the perfect picture to remember all of this by. "She was there one minute," the companion will say in a quavering voice, "and then, well, she just disappeared."

After you died, I kept expecting a letter from you.
    Dear Minrose   Now I'm dead and I hope you're satisfied

Years ago doctors began to tell me that it would be "rational" for me to have a hysterectomy. My mother had ovarian cancer, and so my chances are much higher for getting it. It is hard to diagnose, hence a real killer. Besides, I may be entering menopause ("Do you know when your mother began menopause?" I remember it as early—forty-five—I am older than that now). This is elective surgery. You take your chances. There are cysts now. What next? The one mutated cell: a last parting missive from Erin Taylor.

    Dear Minrose,
    Here's a little something for you. If you take care of it, it will grow.

After my mother's surgery, it took the two doctors three days to tell her that she had cancer. They knew Erin Taylor, and they were afraid of what she would do. They did not want a scene.

"When are you going to tell her?" I would ask. "You mean *he* hasn't told her yet?" the surgeon who was not my mother's friend would say of the gynecologist who was, and shake his head. Asked the same question on his rounds, the gynecologist would express disbelief that the surgeon had said nothing. "I'll talk to him," the former said of the latter. "He did the surgery, so he knows the details." In plain terms the details were that the cancer had spread into the uterus and probably beyond. The poisoned reproductive organs were gone, thanks to a full hysterectomy, but chances were the cancer had cast its nets wider. There was probably no catching up with it.

I didn't know what my mother was going to do when they told her, so I was hanging around the hospital day and night, night and day, waiting. "You are making me so *tired*," she said. "Go home and leave me alone." When one of them did finally tell her, she seemed not to hear. I was standing behind him. My hands were folded like wings over my heart. She threw off the sheets, turned on her side, and slowly pushed herself up to a sitting position in the bed, her lips pursed in pain. "Minrose," she said, "hand me my mirror." As the doctor fled, she snatched up her makeup case on the table beside her bed. She smeared on lipstick (how dark and splattered it looked against her post-surgical pallor) and began to brush her hair, now dingy and matted. "They tell me I have a malignancy," she said, as if I had just come into the room. She unscrewed her eyebrow pencil. "I'm going to have to take chemo. I don't trust these doctors." Then she drew herself some eyebrows that looked oddly like question marks. In the coming years she would speak of what she would call "my malignancy" with a certain amount of pride, as if the cancer were a successful but treacherous child.

My mother's veins were very small. Before every chemother-apy treatment she would call me and cry. Then I would not hear from her for days afterward because she would be too sick to call. After a while the veins started collapsing. I have Erin's Taylor's hands, and her veins. For years now, every six months

I get a not-particularly-reliable blood test with a very reliable-sounding name (a CA 125, which may or may not show abnormal readings if I have gotten ovarian cancer). The technicians always have trouble getting into the vein. I direct them to the more visible vein in my left arm and, with the rubber band pinching my upper arm and my elbow on the cold hard armrest, I think of Mama getting chemotherapy through her feet. In the end she refused the last two treatments. She said it was just not worth it.

That Christmas after my mother's first operation in October, my husband, daughter, and I dragged ourselves down to Mississippi. It was the last thing we wanted to be doing, though we knew we shouldn't feel that way. Four months before, we had moved from one state to another for me to take my first full-time academic job. I had defended my dissertation on the day before classes began, the last day I could possibly do it and get full salary. I had not had time that December to walk through graduation in the cap and gown that had been given to me by the first woman Ph.D. from my alma mater, who had herself recently died of cancer. My husband had given up a well-paying executive position to become an instructor at a quarter of the salary. He had decided to begin doctoral work. Our daughter, who at thirteen had grown up elsewhere, left her friends, and started a new school in a new place, now believed her life was over. In the car we snarled at one another, our angry outbursts fogging up the frosty windshield. On arrival, we got a room at a local motel and put up a plastic tree, under which we sullenly planted our gifts to one another.

On Christmas Eve, my mother, weak and ill, helped me put the Christmas dinner I had cooked on the table. I was planning on talking about the weather over the meal. My mother liked to talk about the weather. She was always wishing for snow. She remembered that once, when she was nine, it actually did snow around Christmas, not exactly *on* Christmas Day, mind you, she would say, but almost, only a few days before. *Really,* she would say, a real snow. And it stuck, for a few hours. When the meal was ready, she sat down at the table. She picked up her fork and, as if the act of picking it up had hurt, burst into tears, kicked her chair back, and ran sobbing from the room. The salesman shook his head as if perplexed, picked up a spoon, and began to take some dressing and gravy. The rest of us looked at one another and began to nibble at celery and olives.

Then we heard a crash. I ran down the hall, opened the door into her bedroom, and found her lying on the bed in the dark. Her hairbrush was on the floor by the door where she'd thrown it. It had big tufts of hair in it. *"I'm going bald,"* she sobbed. *"I'm going to look like an old man. A bald old man."*

She did go totally bald, but I never saw her that way. She wore her wig constantly. Perhaps as a consequence, it was always slightly askew, slipping this way and that, like a hat that was too large. (She also had some turbans she'd wear to sleep in and to go from the shower to the bedroom.) When her hair grew out, it was the color of old snow, and curly.

When the shelf fell on me, they x-rayed my head and neck. When I saw my own skull in the picture, I thought, oddly, that I caught a glimpse of my mother's bald head, as it must have been. It was the first time I saw, unmistakably, my mother in me. This deceptive flesh peeled away, color and cartilage gone, I saw how all this time I'd been riding Erin Taylor's lovely mad bones. Cheek slant, tilt of jaw, skull's curve back, bone on bone.

❖ ❖ ❖

As I sit on the examining table and listen to the doctor telling me about how they have a bit of a problem keeping tabs on my suspicious ovaries and can't get a good look on ultrasound because something is blocking the view, I am trying, without success, to imagine myself bald. There is no doubt in my mind: I would rather have my stomach cut open and my insides taken out, though one does want to ask, what do you *do* with the glistening flesh? How do you tell what's poisonous and what isn't? But I know that there are matter-of-fact answers to these questions. You send it down (always down) to the lab and they send up a report. It's as simple as that. Then they throw the pieces away in a "hazardous materials" garbage can.

LABORATORY REPORT

Pitner, Erin Taylor
Laboratory Number: 83-8674
Hospital Number: 0512228
Date: 10-24-83

MICRO: The sections of the uterus demonstrate a small, well-defined leiomyoma. Fibrous adhesions of the peritoneal surface of the uterus show extensive infiltration by adenocarcinoma. The endometrial polyp is benign. The glands forming it are produced by endothelial cells that show no significant atypia. There is a mild degree of chronic cervicitis. While the Fallopian tubes show no intrinsic lesions both ovaries are extensively involved by adenocarcinoma. The malignant cells grow by adenoid and papillary differentiation. Tumor is present on the peritoneal surface of the ovarian material bilaterally. Psammoma bodies are present in lesion also. The carcinoma also infiltrates the tissue between the Fallopian tube and ovary.

DIAGNOSIS:

1. BILATERAL ADENOCARCINOMA OF OVARIES WITH INVASION
OF MESOSALPINX AND PERITONEUM OF OVARIES 87-8143,
86 & Y4-8143
2. FALLOPIAN TUBES 86-0001
3. UTERUS SHOWING PERITONEAL METASTATIC ADENO-
CARCINOMA 82-8146
4. LEIOMYOMA OF UTERUS 82-8890
5. BENIGN POLYP OF ENDOMETRIUM 84-7381
6. CHRONIC CERVICITIS 83-4300

It is Halloween 1988, the day after my mother's funeral. I am walking in a cold rain around Overton Park Zoo in Memphis, waiting to catch my plane back to Virginia. I can think of nowhere else to go. When I was a girl, my friend's mother took my two friends and me to this zoo. There is a picture of the three of us, silly twelve-year-olds in straw hats, our arms and legs jutting out at odd angles, posed by the zoo photographer, on a park bench. My girlfriends are grinning directly into the camera. I am wearing a cowboy skirt, a hand-me-down from my cousin Lynn, and my white socks are falling down around my loafers. I am cradling the head of a huge stuffed lion, whose rear quarters are in my friends' laps. I am not looking into the camera but rather am absorbed in gazing down at the ragged-faced lion, my arm around it like it was a baby in my lap.

Back then the zoo was notable for three things: a mangy male lion that hollered forth whenever someone came to look at him, some monkeys that chattered and masturbated constantly, and the peacocks parading around with their feathers spread like rows of huge blue-green eyes. I remember the picture-taking, and I remember as I sat there waiting for the flash I was thinking about peacocks. I had followed them around that day, but they had a way of staying just outside the range of touch. Nor would they let me get in front of them to see them in their full splendor head on. When I would go around, they would again turn their backs. They would hop onto fences and into trees. Once, when I was little, my grandfather read me a story in the Memphis newspaper about a peacock from the zoo that turned up in someone's backyard. I would dream of this. I would ask my mother: "Which would you rather wake up in the morning and look out your window and see? A peacock or snow?"

"Snow," she would always say.

When I went to see the farmhouse where Flannery O'Connor lived in Milledgeville, Georgia, I looked for her peacocks. Someone had told me they were still wandering around the old farmplace, but all I saw was an old donkey and a dark row of trees. It was hot and sunny, but everything looked dark; the windows in the old farmhouse were black squares. I thought of how Flannery got out of Georgia in her twenties and began to make a success of her writing. Then, on the way home for Christmas, a heaviness in the arm. She must have known right away what it was, her father having died from lupus. She was riding the train, and she must have watched the winter landscape change, the pure New England snow gradually thawing and giving way to the complicated southern browns and greens, as the arm grew heavier and heavier. Later, her things would have to be sent by saddened friends who knew she would never return. Her mother nursed her through the rest of it, her life, while she wrote about narrow-minded farm women who tried to manage their grown children like cattle or hogs. I look at her steroid-swollen face in the terrible pictures she painted and drew of herself, and I think of how she had to go back and look out over that dark row of trees.

Maybe this is why Flannery ordered herself some pea fowl. They are not what you think they will be, she later wrote. They are beautiful, yes, when they're not molting, but ornery all the time. They won't get out of the road. They have no sense of boundaries; you can't keep them fenced. They will eat anything, and they always want more of what you don't want them to have.

At the zoo I walk with my husband. There are six electrodes stuck to my back with adhesive. They are connected to a unit hooked to a belt at my waist that sends charges to the electrodes. These zap my neck and back just enough so that it almost hurts. By hurting a little on the surface, they are supposed to dull the deeper pain below, perhaps by giving the nerve endings something else to worry about. I have found that, after a while, I can turn the unit up for a stronger current, and then up again. This is because, in the course of the day, I have become accustomed to its sting and can endure more and more. I start each day with the dial on low, and end with it on high.

Our one umbrella drips down the back of my neck. As we come to a cage of baboons, they turn in alarm, throats ballooned out. They begin to make a noise which is something between a laugh and a scream. It is deafening. A female lion in a cage behind me starts to roar. I wonder whether the old male of my youth was her father or grandfather. We stand in the freezing rain between their cages, transfixed by sound.

When my mother died everyone said what a blessing. I want to throw back my head and howl in this baboon language between laughter and outrage. I want to *live* there in a cage in

Overton Park Zoo so that I can balloon out my throat and scream and laugh with the baboons until I die.

One day when I was about fifteen I hit my mother back. After that she stopped hitting me. Slap across my face. Slap across her face, and then: *I hate you   Mama   I wish you were dead.*

Grief is a matter of balance, of rivers and streams and dams and arroyos that flow and hold in time and space. If the balance is altered you can be washed away. You can drown.

My mother's coffin was blue with a border of cornflowers. Her husband selected it. It was a coffin for a country woman who worked in vegetable and flower gardens and wore soft faded muslin aprons and smiled distractedly at her children's antics. My mother would have hated it. As I stood by her gravesite listening to the minister, I expected her at any moment to pop right out of it and roll over outrageously stiff on the wet ground.

MEMENTO MORI

A day of stone.
The audacity of words
crying death
vaunting your name squeezed dry
compressed and pounded
into a gouge of words
brazoned into granite.
Stone words on stone.
Stone.

ERIN CLAYTON PITNER

Minrose daughter of Erin daughter of Minrose daughter of Erin.

Force the stone and wake the lost one, the one who will rise up one bright day and fly away.

I named my daughter Erin Carol to deflect my mother's anger at her too-soon birth. (And who is to say this did not work? How much angrier might my mother have been? Perhaps she would not have ridden the Greyhound bus and sat in the rocking chair, even for a while. Perhaps she would not have sent the little dresses.) The name Carol, by which my daughter is called, was after my friend who left high school in her junior year to take up housekeeping with a new husband and one then two little ones. This first Carol had pearl skin, precise shoulder blades, and black black hair. She and I lived across the street from each other. We would sit at her piano for hours playing simple duets. I couldn't stop looking at her. Sometimes when I would spend the night, I would wait until she had gone to sleep so that I could look at her more carefully under the streetlight that came through her window. She loved yellow roses. She died at age twenty-one, along with her two baby girls, when her father took the carload of them out onto the highway in front of an oncoming car.

The rest of her family being either dead, in the hospital with multiple injuries, or paralyzed by horror, I was asked to help out, to go to the house to pull out of Carol's closet something for her to wear in her coffin. We were the same size and wore each other's clothes, or perhaps I should say I wore hers. She had stunning and unusual clothes because her mother was an artist who could sew. I pulled out dress after dress, many of which I myself had worn. Because the living Carol was beautiful and angular and always in motion, everything she wore had seemed somehow grander than it was. On her, cotton became silk, a simple shift became a goddess's drape. For the dead Carol, nothing seemed right. The house was in the kind of mess one makes when getting off on a short trip with young children, wet diapers on the bathroom floor, bed unmade, remnants of breakfast still on the kitchen table. I tried to pick things up, neaten the place for the husband who would one day soon have to come home to this. I do not remember walking out of the little house, but I must have. I don't remember whether I chose a dress, much less which one. When I returned to college that spring, I began at midterm to sit in on courses in absurdism and existentialism. I began to smoke dope with professors who wore black and gathered sad students like squirrels hoarding nuts against the winter snows.

My daughter, it now occurs to me, carries the names of two women who were unlucky.

MIRROR OF REMEMBRANCE

The glass darkened
and the image shattered.
But the broken years slowly
begin to heal themselves,
as time splints up
the fragments
of the pattern.

And now when April comes,
I see you again,
running down the mirrored edges
of my dreams,
with yellow roses slipping

from your black hair.
Each tender petal
floating
lucent in the air
of early spring.

No fear of wintry darkness
may shadow the clear reflected sunlight
of your eyes.
No disenchantment of the years
may mock nor change the perfect image
of your smile.

ERIN CLAYTON PITNER

A friend, age twenty-nine, tells me about her mother who died
several years ago of brain cancer, like others in the Los Alamos
area for reasons never determined. Her mother was not yet
fifty, my friend says, and she wanted her ashes scattered from
one of the peaks of the Sangre de Cristo Mountains outside of
Santa Fe. Every year on the date of her mother's death my
friend climbs back to where she threw her mother's ashes up
in the air and watched them fall like cottonwood fluff. She can
still can see shards of her mother's bones lying on the rocks.
But fewer every year, she says, fewer as time passes.

Erin the daughter mourned Minrose the mother years before
Minrose died. My grandmother had become bedridden and se-
nile and had been taken from the red brick house with its
sturdy foundation and put in a local nursing home. When it
was determined that the family house needed to be sold to pay

my grandmother's expenses, my grandmother being obviously unable ever to return to it, my mother raged for weeks. She accused her brother of being mercenary and told him that, whatever else he did, he should not—absolutely could not— allow a for-sale sign in the yard because then just *anybody* would think they could buy the house. She spent hours marking the names of people in the telephone book she might possibly be willing to sell the house to and then spent more hours calling and telling them so. She ran an antique dealer off the front porch with a broom.

"I won't have just *anybody* living here," she told me on the phone. "I just won't have it. And no antique dealers. Some people will do *anything* for a living."

When the house was sold to some perfectly nice people from The North whose name didn't sound reassuringly Anglo Saxon and who eventually put the monster pot that looked like a space ship in the front yard and painted all the trim red, my mother had a fit.

"How *could* you do such a thing!" she screamed at her brother. "How could you sell *my* mother's house to *Northerners?* They don't know the first thing about a house like this."

It was strange to think of the stronger-than-a-tornado house belonging to people who thought of it as a place to put a red pot. I thought of the summer nights before the salesman came to take us away, how in the dusk of coming evening the children would take over the big swing and make it squeak and go higher and higher by pushing as hard as we could with our feet until the grownups said to slow up, the swing was too old for that. How, when the shade came over in late afternoon, my plump little grandmother would stand in the brooding half-light like a queen with her scepter, watering her petunia bed with a garden hose. My grandfather had died in that house.

The newspaper account of his death says he died at the hospital after suffering a heart attack at home, but Eva said she heard him shout her name and then fall, and when she got upstairs he rose up from his bed and fell right into her arms, scrabbling at her with his fingernails like he was trying to climb a tree (which is more feasible than one might think given the fact of his scrawniness and Eva's height and weight—she weighed almost twice as much as he). Then he turned his elbows in and folded like a box, and she let him down easy to the floor so he wouldn't bang his head. He was dead then, she insisted, dead as he could be.

His coffin with him in it was kept in the dining room, propped on top of the large buffet, an odd place for a corpse it seems to me now, and even then, when such familiarities with the dead were more common, I couldn't help thinking about large cuts of meat I'd seen in exactly the same position on the buffet and with the same sense of heavy waiting. I as the oldest grandchild (I was thirteen) was the one selected to stay overnight in the house with my living grandmother and my grandfather's body. Mama told me to get my toothbrush and go take care of my grandmother. "This will be the worst night of her life," my mother said. She had just gotten off the phone downstairs in my grandparent's house calling and telling people the news. She was crying, but she was telling it like it was lemon meringue pie.

My grandmother was upstairs in her room. When I went in, she was standing in front of her dresser so that I could see her back and her front at the same time. My grandmother had loose skin. It had its own way of moving, lying in rolls or swinging nice and free across the undersides of her arms, her throat, her bosoms that lay flat and long like sausages under her slips. She had pretty hair. Everybody said so. Brown and silver in front. She was wearing it in a kind of bun with a wavy silvery puff over her eyes, which she was brushing back.

Now she stops the brushing and looks flat at me in the mirror. She still has the brush in her hand, and the skin on her arm is dangling like a piece of rope.

"Minrose," she says, "I don't know. I just really don't know."

I'm not sure what she doesn't know, but I'm not asking. The mirror pulls at her face, and it seems stretched out too long. I'm crying now, and she goes to her drawer and pulls out a handkerchief with "M" for Minrose on it and hands it to me. She does not bother with one for herself. She sits down in her rocking chair and starts to rock. The chair squeaks out as usual its song that sounds like katydid, katydid. She looks out the window at the top of the fig tree next to the house with its big old elephant ears for leaves. Her whole face is wet, as if she's crying from every pore.

I blow my nose, and we sit there crying and rocking, with me hearing the katydid, katydid creak of her chair going back and forth, and our knees barely touching when we both rock forward at the same time. The broken slat in my grandfather's chair is jabbing me in the back like a knife, but it feels good somehow. *Amo, amas, amat, amamus, amatis, amant.* She's not saying a word now, but I know she's thinking *amo, amas, amat,* and it's making her cry even worse.

Now she gets up and goes over to her bed and crawls in, clothes and all. She curls up on her side and puts the cover right up to her nose and gets very still. The sun is high, and nothing looks right. I go to the other side of the bed and crawl in too. Her back is to me but I can feel her flesh leaning toward me so I just turn toward her and fold myself up against her back, the way I used to do at night when I was the bat and she was the cave.

That night my grandfather, who had always walked all over the place while everyone else was asleep, didn't let up. He walked the house all night long. The upstairs had a large square hall in the middle, and I kept hearing the wood boards scrape and creak as he walked between his bedroom and his study. He sounded restless, ready to go somewhere but being held up somehow, like the times when he would pace in his Sunday suit waiting for all of us to get ready for church. I pulled the sheet over my head and did not move.

You read about these sorts of things happening, but you don't really believe them; they just make a good story. Until that night I believed that when people die they are dead—they are gone from this world—but my grandfather's walking taught me that a person doesn't just fly away like my fledgling hummingbirds. There is a flutter, a hesitation, the duration of which is contingent on the burden of the dead one's desire to stay.

Between my grandfather's footsteps, I fall into a sleep that takes the shape of a long dark tunnel. I am thinking that I am alone in the house. The house is dark, but as I wander from room to room, I see that there are babies tucked into beds and corners, in rows on the living room floor, babies everywhere, like the wounded after the big tornado. These petal-soft babies have on little handmade dresses, so I think they are girls, though they may be long-ago babies from the time when boys also wore such things. As I stand guard over these babies, who

seem to multiply as I watch, the coals in the living room fire-
place begin to glow a deeper and deeper orange and then tumble out like boulders until flames lick the gauze curtains at the
windows. I cry for help but everyone responsible is outside
sledding, though in Mississippi it never snows enough for that.
Red coals fall like stars, and chairs and tables burn and melt. I
know I should save these tender-faced babies, but when sparks
fall on their little dresses like wistful blossoms, I see that nothing can be done.

I wonder whether the Northerners hear steps at night in the
big hall. Do they hear you walking, Mother, and what do they
think?

My mother walked hard and fast. "Why does she walk so
loud?" my little daughter would say when we visited. "I don't
like the way Mimi walks."

(Down the hall, here she comes. One child cringing in
the bed. One in the closet. I'm older and wiser. I have a chair
wedged under my doorknob.)

In her later years my mother walked for exercise. She did not
walk on sidewalks or in the streets like most people. She
seemed to have an invisible path in mind when she began, and
she walked straight through people's yards, back and front,
without looking right or left and with what seemed to be a
quickened sense of purpose, the way a dog will trot faster and
faster, not acknowledging your friendly call, when it is lost.
People would peer out their windows and shake their heads or
sit on their patios and porches and look startled by the intru-
sion of Erin Taylor speeding through their backyards as if she
were on some urgent errand. Sometimes she would stop and

pick a flower or a piece of fruit as if it belonged to her. Dogs would bark and cats would scurry.

Over her later life she had several dogs. Her favorite was a blond curly-haired mutt she named after the movie star Benji. Far from star material himself, Benji was smelly and had bad breath. His coat was thin and he had eczema. He inevitably got into fights with other dogs on these jaunts because she seldom leashed him and because he, like her, had no feeling for boundaries.

FANTASY

We buried you deep.
Above you many layers of leaf mold
many seasons of grief.
All sizes and shapes of you—
soulless, they say
denying love unbound by earth or heaven.

We piled stones on your head
to keep you tethered to eternity
safely sealed in blackness of time
forgotten.
Yet you rise and roam the moon
with me.
Diana with her hounds
unleashed.
Free.

ERIN CLAYTON PITNER

When Mama got crazier, she began to walk in fewer and fewer clothes. First she started walking in her bathrobe—she called it her brunch coat, which made it in her mind, I guess, a more acceptable walking garment. Toward the end, she took to walking in her nightgowns. She also walked faster and faster. A few days before we committed her to the first mental hospital, I chased her all over the neighborhood trying to get her to put on some clothes. She was in her flowered cotton gown, stockings flapping at her ankles, the untied laces of her sensible walking shoes flying.

"Quit following me!" she would turn block by block and yell at me. "Leave me alone. Go away. I know what you want. You want to lock me up."

Sometimes now in my dreams I am walking as fast as I can behind my mother, calling out to her and trying to catch up. She looks fearfully over her shoulder and walks faster and faster until I fall behind. Finally she disappears in the distance, brunch coat flying, her unraveled stockings breezing behind like the tails of somebody's lost kite.

CORTEGE

Late afternoon
and I out walking the world
blue-hazed in the chill of autumn
the deserted streets crying the bitterness
of gold and crimson.
No other sound
but the steady muffled thrumming
of the darkness
falling behind my footsteps
block by block.

ERIN CLAYTON PITNER

In commitment proceedings in Mississippi, the normal procedure is that the sheriff's deputies (how many depends on how actively crazy you are) come out and get you. They serve the commitment papers on you and then they take you to jail. There you remain for sometimes as long as a week while psychiatrists and social workers examine you to assess whether you are really crazy or whether your family is just trying to get rid of you for one reason or another. At least so it was in the 1980s.

The first time my mother is committed:

Alarmed by her strange letters and phone calls, I come down to visit, take one look at her, and see only bones and hair and eyes, as if she has peeled herself back to the last nonfleshy remnants of herself. I tell the salesman that something has to be done. We decide to bring her in ourselves instead of having the deputies come out to the house. It is arranged for her to be held in the psychiatric wing of the local hospital instead of going to jail. The first commitment is a family effort, one of our only mutual projects, in fact. It is the salesman, my brother, my husband, and I against my mother.

We plot and plan. We tell the roofing crew across the street not to worry when they see us carrying a screaming woman from the house. We jump my mother as she prepares for a nap and pick her up by her arms and legs and place her kicking and screaming in the car. The roofers watch open-mouthed from their roof. We do not take her to jail. Instead we drive her to the hospital and get her into a room that has been set aside for her. We feel enormously relieved that this has been so easily accomplished. Three men and a woman getting my seventy-five-pound mother to go somewhere she doesn't want to go. (Is the anorexia caused by the chemo? I ask her doctors.

Definitely not, they say. Absolutely nothing to do with the chemotherapy, they say.)

As we cluster in the hospital corridor, the door to her room bursts open. To our horror, she comes out screaming that she is not going to stay in her room or in the hospital. We ask the nurses to do something, and they respond that they can't do a thing. The hospital will provide a room for crazy Erin Taylor, but she can't be held there against her will. She will have to go to jail if she doesn't calm down.

"You've locked me in!" she screams as she tries to open the heavy double doors leading out of the hospital psych ward. She is so rickety from eating only a few green beans a day (out of her boundless supply of cans and pots of them) that she can't open the big doors. She storms back down the hall toward me brandishing her purse from side to side. *"Minrose, you're responsible for this. You're the one. I know it. You'll pay for this, young lady!"*

She charges up and down the corridor, hair plastered to her head, barefooted, clutching her purse, which she swings at me in repeated attempts to hit me over the head as she strides by.

"Yes," I lie. "You're locked in. You have to stay here until we can get help for you."

For days Erin Taylor storms up and down the hall of the hospital psych ward thinking she is locked in. She screams and walks. Growls and walks. Curses and walks. She swings her purse and knocks into people as if they are not there. She walks all day and all night, claiming every inch of the space she thinks she is locked into. I sit hunched over in a waiting room chair, my head bowed because I do not want to see this, watching her feet go back and forth, back and forth.

* * *

When it was time for the people from up North to move in, I came down to help Mama pack up my grandparents' house. She lingered over everything—chipped dishes, the doorstop that looked like a cat, Minrose's old hats. "Do you think I could wear these?" she asked me, trying on one after another of her mother's flower- and fruit-covered hats. In her mother's flamboyant hats she gazed with interest at herself in her mother's mirror above the dresser with its walnut breasts. Minrose's hairbrush, fingernail scissors, hand mirror, comb were still neatly placed on the marble top. Somehow the hats had looked right on my full-faced, full-bodied little grandmother; they had balanced her figure. On Erin Taylor, thin even then, they looked like a series of Welcome Wagon baskets.

"Come on, Mama," I said in my schoolteacher's voice, "or we're never going to get this done."

When we finally had everything packed and it was time to go, I breathed a sigh of relief. I had been there all week, and I was ready to get back home. I was missing my graduate seminars, and I had friends covering my classes and neighbors looking after my daughter after school. I was worried that something somewhere was going to go badly wrong and it would be my fault. The spring before, I had left my daughter, nine years old, in the yard for twenty minutes to run to the bus stop to pick up my husband. It was the first time I had left her at home alone. Playing in the backyard, she stepped onto a yellow jacket hole. I had instructed her that if a stinging insect came near to stand still and not run or swat at it. When several dozen rancorous yellow jackets came roaring out of their disturbed home, she stood obediently still and let them sting her before thinking the better of her mother's bad advice. Upon returning home, I found her sobbing in the bathtub of a neighbor covered in stings, welts, and baking soda.

Mama and I walked out into the backyard. It was cold, that moldy wet cold you get on an afternoon in Misssissippi in November. She sighed and looked out over the dead flower beds. I opened the car door for her. In that moment something in her face opened and closed. "The flowers," she said, turning to look out over the yard, and slammed the car door shut. "We can't leave the *flowers*. Get the shovel."

Iris, jonquils, narcissus. You want them all. On this dark November day we dig for bulbs and roots and rhizomes. We turn over the cold ground and scratch about, like dogs on the scent of long-lost bones.

There you say   there's one.   *Here?* I say.   Yes *there* you say. And it sounds like music, your voice.

We dig up the whole backyard, huge beds of flowers planted God knows when but still alive, bulbs clotted with red clay, hard and cold on the outside but utterly alive, we know, inside, thrown in paper bags and put in the car to be taken across town and transplanted in your yard. (And mine. These are my flowers too that I have taken, and left behind.) Our breath clouds the air. Our cheeks are red and cold to the touch. We are utterly happy.

We forget the clematis because it is November and it has died back. The next spring, months after the new people have moved in, my mother goes back for the clematis vine—just marches herself into the yard and starts digging it up. No explanations. No apologies.

This is what I remember. I can feel it all so deliciously. The wet clay. The you and me. The way our breath held like smoke in the cold air before disappearing.

Evidence of these events, however, is to the contrary. (This means, of course, that I cannot be trusted.)

THE INGATHERING

November
and the slow unwinding
of days
the long light
slipping
into silence
reluctant to leave the warmth
of the sun.
The fields almost barren now
waiting
for the ingathering
the late sweet corn gleaned and stored
before frost.
Dreams too
hidden beneath the withered husks of summer
sweet as the yellow corn gathered in
hoarded
against winter.

ERIN CLAYTON PITNER

It is hard to tell the truth. The memory plays tricks. We can dream things that never happened. Things happen that cannot be dreamed. In a letter I found in my box of old photographs, my mother writes that she was alone on that cold November day when the house was finally closed up:

I've never told you the half of it—the last day in November
was cold & rainy—completely dreary & depressing. I had
to walk thru to see that everything was gone & then I sat
for a long time on the stairs in the hall. It was hard to leave
& there was no one at home either.

I came through that period & closed the door.

But this happened about 3 weeks ago & I swear it is
true. One night I had the most vivid dream. I dreamed I
went back to the house and walked up to the sunroom windows. I stood and like a child pressed my face against the
glass. It was wonderful—everything was perfect. The sun
was shining so brightly in the sun room. . . . Through the
open door to the bedroom I saw Mother's bed all made up
with a beautiful white bedspread. She was not there but you
know what was lying on that bed? A white lace handkerchief and a fan. This room too was flooded with sunlight. I
woke up almost feeling I could touch it all. There was such
a feeling of happiness and peace that I can't describe it.
Everything was "all right." This feeling stayed with me for
a long time. I've never had a more real dream.

Love to all,
Mama

Now as I read this letter, I wonder whether anything I have
written is true. When did we dig the flowers, Mother? Was it
the day before the last day? The week before?

When I visited my grandmother's grave for the first time,
I was shocked to see my own name on her gravestone. Minrose. I felt as if my breath had been sucked away by those
seven letters carved in that particular order on the big gravestone. (This may seem odd to most people who see and hear
their own names used with a variety of human referents, but I

have never seen *Minrose* written anywhere, much less on a gravestone, unless it referred to my grandmother or myself.) I felt I was looking down on my own grave.

My grandmother died quietly and slowly after having already left us for another place. The leaving started when Minrose was deprived of her means of travel, her gray Plymouth that looked like a swollen toadstool on wheels. Even as she had grown in girth, she had shrunk in height over the years, having been about five feet two in her prime; her head was barely visible behind the Plymouth's massive wheel as she, older now and so less inclined to worry that she might die prematurely, went cavorting through stop signs and gaily passing cars on Main Street because she was late for her beauty shop appointment. So one late afternoon after work, Erin Taylor's brother—whose childhood nickname, "Boy Blue," wouldn't do in adulthood and so he had become "Son" to his mother and "Brother" to mine—marched up to the back door of the house and regretfully asked her to turn over the car keys.

She did so reluctantly, but sweetly, as was her nature. I was then in college, and when I would come home to visit, she would get me to drive her here and there and sometimes no place at all, just driving out on the highway and up and down the streets of town so she could look at people's yards. Sometimes, she told me, she would go out to the garage and just sit behind the wheel, and turn it as best she could. And sometimes, at night, very late at night, she told me she would retrieve her extra set of keys she had had the foresight to hide in the hatbox with her red cherry hat, as she called it, and take a drive, that is, before the Plymouth itself was sold.

Then, all fun gone, sweet Minrose turned queer. In contrast

to her daughter, who would come to eat less and less, she ate more and more. She had started to eat sweets after her Stewart died. Now she had to have several of Eva's apricot cakes a week.

AFTERWARDS

Now I know why you ate and ate,
gathering your strength about you
like a great warm cloak to ward off
the frigid onslaught of time.

Dad died in August and all of winter
lay ahead—a vast abyss to be bridged
alone, a lesion of hunger like a hollow tooth
clamoring to be warmed and soothed and restored.

I crave peppermints and lemon custard
thick with cream.
The bittersweet twinge of dark chocolate,
your favored treat, suffices at midnight . . .
but nothing fills the void.

ERIN CLAYTON PITNER

The old hungry queer Minrose had become convinced that Eva was waiting for her to have a stroke and become mute so that Eva could torture her and steal her possessions. Perhaps, she speculated, Eva might put rat poisoning or drugs in one of her apricot cakes. "If I have a stroke," she would instruct me in a whisper from her spindle bed, looking like a plumped-up version of Miss Erin in her white gown, *"don't let Eva take care of me. She'll poison me. She'll do things to me, and I won't be able to tell. I know she's hated me all these years. And I don't* know why. I've been good to her. I paid her social security and gave her all my old hats."

Eva, who was a member in good standing of St. Paul Methodist Church, the Eastern Star, and the Heroines of Jericho, and therefore not accustomed to accusations of mayhem, would shake her head and get the tight lip. "Sick and tired of this business," she'd mutter ominously. "If I'd been going to kill her, would've done it a long time ago and saved myself a whole lot of trouble." Eva had cut back her hours because of her legs, and when I was an undergraduate in the college down the road, she had an operation on one leg to pull out the infected veins and "try to clean things up," as the doctor put it. Both of her legs had gotten progressively worse over the years. By now they were ulcerated and smelled like pus.

Nov. 9, 1965

BIRTHDAY WISHES

May this birthday be
Especially glad for you,
May you know the pleasures
Of all your dreams come true;
May you have a long life
Filled with joy and cheer —
Growing ever brighter
Year after happy year!

Dear Minrose —
My leg is doing fine now since I have worn out 5 cast. I am still going to the Dr with it I have faith that it is going to get well of coarse it take time most of the swelling is gone and it have not bled in a while so I have hope I can

see that is an improve. Thinking of you on your birthday.
Hope it is a happy one. We got through both club with
chicken salad and Gemme chocolate cake cheese ball olives
and pineapple sherbert. . . . We are still making approcot
cake I have made so many untill I made one in my sleep one
night. . . . you know what I mean. I cant wait to see you I
guess they have wrote and told you about my only Brother
dying that is the last member of my family but I am still
thinking about I have a lots to be thankful for that it is as
well with me as it is But you know I cant help but be hurt
some because I was un able to go to see the remains of him
But the Lord know best so I just ask his will be on earth
as it is in heaven and I am satisfied

    Will write you again remember I love you a lots
    Happy birthday

Eva.

P.S. I had to use all my paper. Stamp is to expenciv. (Smile)

Jan. 20, 1966

Dear Minrose
Just a note to tell you that I came through the operation
fine and am doing fine I am walking end the hospital. The
operation started about eight oclock Tuesday and I got back
to bed just before one oclock so I was real tired I have been
feeling just tired and worn out but I feel fine to day I call the
school house to ask them to help me make the blood they
had to give me up I hope they will that will sav me a lots of
money I do hope that I am on the road to recover now my
leg look like I have been in a fight and I got stab Look like
I am realy paying Dr Knife to butcher me up. (smile) I hope
it is worth it Well you take good care of you self and I hope

I will see you the next time around Tuesday morning when
I got up out here the first thag I saw was snow but it did not
last very long They tell me it is very cold out side to day I
dont know because I am on the end side looking Out. Smile.

Will write you again just wanted you to hear it from me
that i am fine

rember I love you a lots

Eva Lee Miller

Two years later a blood clot from one leg traveled to Eva's
brain. She died at the hospital at 8:30 P.M. on October 17, 1968,
almost exactly twenty years before Erin Taylor would take her
last ambulance ride. Eva was fifty-eight. She had worked for
my grandparents almost half of her life. She left her husband
Hiram, a stepdaughter, four stepgrandchildren, and two step-
great-grandchildren.

I could not go to Eva's funeral because I was covering
the civil rights demonstrations in Atlanta, the southeastern
division headquarters of United Press International. It was
six months after King had been shot dead—I'd taken the call
from the UPI Memphis office—and the streets were on fire.
Walking the streets and sitting in the balcony of Ebenezer Bap-
tist Church taking notes during the hymn singing, I cried
for Eva. My mother sent me the "Obsequies of the Late Mrs.
Eva Lee Miller" held at St. Paul Methodist Church, in which
special tribute was given to Eva by the Heroines of Jericho.
My mother told me how sad it was, how beautiful and sad was
the singing.

Eva was buried in the "colored" part of the cemetery. She
had a "policy man" who, I knew, had collected a dollar a week

from her for burial insurance ever since I'd known her. He was a white man who chewed tobacco and had Grecian Formula hair, and he came to the black part of town every Friday afternoon, on payday. "He *preys* on those people," my mother would say. I'd been at Eva's a couple of times when he'd come. She said he was robbing her blind but she didn't want to be caught short. Once when I was at her house visiting during my college years, she told him she didn't have the dollar. "You can't get blood out of a turnip," she said and told him to come back on Monday. I reached into my purse, but she flashed her eyes at me and I put it down. It was my mother who bought Eva's tombstone, which was later stolen from the grave, so that, years later, when I would come to visit her resting place, I would be unable to find it.

Without Eva, my hungry grandmother had to go into the nursing home. She was there for a long time, and later stopped being hungry and still later stopped knowing where she was. My mother terrorized the nursing home. She visited her mother every evening around the supper hour, stalked the nurses and nursing aides for imagined oversights, sniffed for the odor of stale urine, which she said was a dead giveaway of shoddy care, prowled the corridors for signs of uncleanliness or disfunction, called in the aides for this and that. A shifting of the patient. More Jell-O. A change of diaper. A sponge bath. They rolled their eyes, whispered behind their hands.

"Smell the urine?" my mother would say in a loud voice, as we passed the nurses' station. "It's a disgrace. They do not keep the place clean. You can always tell by the smell."

Unaware of all the trouble that was being caused on her

behalf, Minrose lived on, often holding herself as if guarding something precious.

SUNDAY AFTERNOON AT THE HOSPICE

Words flicker and die on my lips.
My throat is a furnace stoked
with tears unshed.

I peer beyond the dark ruin of your eyes
for a glint, a spark
and find broad vistas of sunlight untarnished
and wide terraced lawns.

All is the same.
The house waiting for me to begin
the long leisurely descent toward afternoon
and you on the porch late
smiling to yourself the familiar peace
of day's end.

You waiting for me.

ERIN CLAYTON PITNER

When Minrose finally did die in her mid eighties—much to everyone's relief, her own included perhaps—Erin Taylor could not stop crying and talking about her mother. "I don't know what's wrong with me," she said on the phone. "It's like I lost myself."

"Oh, heavens," my aunt said when I came down to try to cheer Mama up, "everybody's mother dies sometime. It is too much the way she's carrying on. It's not normal."

"There's something wrong with your mother," the salesman

said. "She just can't get back on the straight and narrow again. She just can't get straight."

It is true. Something has happened. Erin Taylor, now in her fifties, can't get back to flat biscuits and cornbread. She is no longer a daughter, and she is tired of being a wife. She won't get straight.

WIFE OF THE CANDIDATE

On her lips
the grimace of fresh scarlet
miming the grin he is famous for —
his head cocked
with paw outstretched
oblivious of all
save the need to be seen
and stroked
as he approaches
the crowd.

Faint as old bruises
her blue eyes half-closed
refuting the gaze
of the camera . . .
smiling.

ERIN CLAYTON PITNER

It is now the late 1970s. Erin Taylor is a social worker specializing in helping abused children, especially adolescent girls, in a job at the shelter, where she may or may not have been actually employed. She is mourning her mother Minrose both before and after her mother's death. She is taking classes in creative writing and beginning to write better and better poems. She is also taking sleeping pills and tranquilizers, talking about leaving her husband, and having accidents.

She calls in refills, and the pharmacist calls her back to say no. From what I gather, these are genteel exchanges, as if she is ordering fruits or vegetables which aren't in season. Erin Taylor, you refilled these last week. I can't—mustn't—fill them again so soon. Oh Sam don't worry. I dropped them down the commode, all of them. Down they went like pearls off a broken strand. Now send me some more on out here. Of course I'm not taking too many.

Meanwhile: her car has begun to take on a life of its own and started running off the road for no apparent reason. I don't understand, she says. Maybe something is wrong with the steering. A neighbor stops by and finds her passed out on the living room sofa. I took some medicine, she says. Maybe too much. Maybe an allergic reaction. I don't know. Things seem so strange.

The salesman is still gone most of the week, but often she is not there to fix him a meal when he comes home. "I'm afraid of him," she whispers on the phone. "I've got to get out of here." (She is writing, I now discover from her dusty notebooks, poems about men who kill and maim women.)

She decides she wants what she calls a trial separation and rents a place to live in the university town fifty miles away. Then she sets out to search for a mentor, as if she is looking for a dress for a party. "I need a mentor," she tells me on the phone. "I don't have one and I need one. These days everyone has a mentor."

At this point Erin Taylor, called Erin by her new literary friends, is an older woman whose car keeps running off the road and who writes passionately about her mother. She asks several of her professors, all men, to be her mentor. They say, okay, sure. They say sure they'll talk to her whenever they have time, just drop by during office hours.

She takes a writing workshop from a famous southern poet who is a visiting professor. Among her things are two poems with his comments. On the first, entitled "My Mother's Room," beside the first line of the poem the query: "omit?" In the second stanza, the word *no* circled and again the query: "omit?" At the end of the poem: "This is very good." On the second poem, which is about her mother's death and the breakup of the family house, "Omit" (no question mark) with lines through four lines. In the margin: "This is powerful! Again, I am struck by your bold, imaginative phrases and images. It is not too long, though I would cut those lines I've marked; they're unnecessary and more prosaic than most of the others. You don't need a mentor. Just write!"

SECOND BLOOMING

The clematis is a rusty thicket of leaves
staining the garden.
A single marigold on a withered stalk
is an aging chanteuse
with tinseled head and tarnished throat.
Deep in the environs of November
a pale pink althea is flouting the dark.
Flushed and bemused by the flagrance
of her sudden blooming.

ERIN CLAYTON PITNER

Feb. 10, 1977

Dear Mama,

Received your letter & poem today. I thought the poem
was very good—excellent, superb!! I think you should
start shipping your stuff off to anybody & everybody &
see what happens. Are you afraid of a rejection slip? Don't
be. Everybody gets those—even Faulkner. And, for goodness sake, start at the top and work down. Also, be sure to
read the part in *Writers' Market* about rights. Don't give
anybody "all rights." You might want to publish a collection
later.

Love, Minrose

When I wrote this letter, I was thinking about how my
mother was translating her life into another language. She had
begun to keep a notebook called "Words to Keep," in which
she listed words that especially struck her. She was reading the
dictionary as if it were a good novel. In her poems she bran-
dished nouns and verbs, adjectives and adverbs like flaming
swords. Her poems felt hot on the page. I had begun to wonder
whether she were having an affair.

CERES SPEAKS

Deep in the earth's belly
I hear the first twinge
of the oarlock and the boat
bumping ashore.

His big black barge is richly appointed
with jeweled scepters of onyx
and great black pearls to brandish

before her eyes like Morpheus
enthralling her back for one more night
in his arms.

This time I followed her to the bottom
of winter, those icelocked caverns
of the heart thrumming
to the dark muffled cadence
of the river.
Earth and sky flash by,
the dark and light of it
over and under and back again,
bearing her away from me
with every stroke of the oar.

When spring roused her,
I became the clod of earth
pillowing her head, a lodestone
to lure her back from
the cold dark somnolence of time.
Her seasons rise now and throb
in my throat. Better veins
icelocked forever —
than this interminable thawing.

ERIN CLAYTON PITNER

*An affair   you think you know so much   how to begin when the end
was so near   that was the question   it was too late then   by then it
was too late   the worm had already turned   and deep down I knew it*

Today I look across my desk at a sixty-year-old woman graduate student who is worried about getting an academic job. She

knows she has waited too long. I look into her lined face—she has dressed up for this meeting, I can see that, and she has her list of careful questions to ask me.

For a moment she hesitates. Then she clears her throat and begins. She wants to write her dissertation on this and that, and she wants me to direct it, that is, if I'm willing. She knows she's, well, a bit late in life, maybe too late, to be undertaking such a thing. But will I do it?

How late is too late? Eva's fifty-eight years? Erin's sixty-seven?

I want to lean over to touch this woman's shoulder, which looks, I suddenly notice, braced, as if for a blow. I want to tell her that it's not too late. You can be too early as easily as you can be too late. I want her to get to the other side of too late, draw the one ragged breath you draw after a long spell of crying when you know that you've cried enough for this time. I want her to feel something turn toward the moment.

Will I do it? Is it too late?

"Yes," I say.

VII

Thursday December 4, 1930

I know all those states and capitals at last. There were 14 states and 14 capitals to learn. I studed them last night and just now. I think I know them pretty well. I wish she had just given 7 states and 7 capitals to learn.

Friday December 5, 1930

Nothing ecciting happened today. I wrote a letter to Santa Claus and daddy sent it up the chimmley. That is all I have to say today.

Sunday December 7, 1930

I forgot to write anything yesterday. This morning when I got up Mother had already gotten up and gone to the Post Office to mail a letter. I couldn't imageine where she was. But when she came back she told me where she had been.

Monday December 8, 1930

I thought I was going to get to write some more yesterday but I didnt. Boy Blue was teaching me how to ride his bicycle and I fell off and hurt my ankle. David Baker didn't mean to and kicked it this morning and I mean it hurt too.

Tuesday December 9, 1930

Uncle Van and aunt Sibil are here to see us. Daddy was helping me with my arithmetic and he sure did fuss at me about it. I don't guess he meant anything by it but I didn't like it much. Goodbye until tomorrow.

VIII

palingenesis: birth over again; regeneration. Doctrine of successive rebirths.
palimpsest: parchment or tablet that has been written or inscribed 2 or 3 times, previous text or texts having been imperfectly erased and remaining, therefore, still partially visible.

In a ninety-nine-cent spiral notebook with a photograph of a giant snowdrift on the front cover, Erin the poet, sometime during her late fifties to early sixties, inscribed the title: "Alphabet of Words to Keep." Inside her snowdrift notebook, she wrote each letter of the alphabet across the top of every third or fourth page, and under their first letter she neatly tucked her chosen words to keep (and their definitions), like babes put down for a winter nap.

palladium: 1. in ancient Greece or Rome, any statue of Greek goddess Pallas Athena; specif. the legendary statue in Troy on the preservation of which the safety of the city was supposed to depend. 2. anything supposed to ensure the safety of something; safeguard.

The date on Erin's notebook is 1980. (I know this only because an Olympic competitor in a USA red, white, and blue

snowmobile is parked on the side of the drift, atop the motto
"Let's Win in 1980.") It is after Erin's departure from the home
for abused children and after her failure to get another job in
social work, the profession she had so diligently prepared herself for by obtaining a second degree and completing countless
hours of unpaid field work.

July 10, 1976

Dear Erin,

I would like to convey to you the sincere and deep thanks of
the Three Rivers Regional Ministry Policy Board for your
one year of voluntary service with us. The board passed a
resolution expressing their appreciation to you, and asked
that I relay their gratitude to you.

Your time, your talents, the gift that you are as a person,
these helped our regional ministry immensely, and they were
of real service to many people. We do appreciate it!

It is still B.C., Before Cancer, and the height of poetry writing, marriage dissatisfaction, and running off the road. It is the
year that Erin the poet goes to work, unbelievably, for the U.S.
Park Service at the Natchez Trace. (At the time, I can't believe
she can get a government job—what about background
checks?—much less hold one, but she does both, which just
goes to show how little I know.) Erin greets travelers along the
Trace, gives directions to Indian mounds and bathrooms, and
walks a half mile twice each day to raise and lower the flag, the
latter task being her favorite part of the job, she says, because
it keeps her in shape and makes her feel patriotic. She has her
federal government paycheck and benefits, and she is wearing
her weighty metal nameplate, which I found in the top drawer

of the walnut-breasted dresser along with the hat pins from another era.

In the midst of these noisy comings and goings of living
travelers and the silent ebb and flow of displaced spirits of the
Chickasaw and early wayfarers murdered along that most dangerous of paths, my mother is thinking about words. I imagine her in the Park Service uniform of green polyester sitting
behind the counter at the Natchez Trace Parkway Center
flanked by oaks and sweetgum trees, sneaking peeks at her
Webster's as if she is shoplifting jewelry she will later sell on
the street, scribbling words on bits of stolen government paper.
Some of her words tucked loosely into the snowdrift notebook
are written on the back of scraps of government memos, park
press releases, animal identification cards ("type of animal,"
"location of animal," "description of animal"), and topographic
maps.

They are a ragtag crew, these words, but they are indeed
words to keep. Melancholy words and frisky words. Words
like pliers that open things up. Words like hammers that nail
things down. Words that fly away and words that stay. Words
looking for a poem.

bubble & squeak: cabbage & pots. fried together.
flint-knapping: the ancient art of chipping weapon points.
(Indian lore)
greenheart: tropical trees; hardness and resistance to blight &
decay; the wood. (greenhearted?)
hypertonic: abnormally high tension or tone, esp. of muscles.
hypocenter: point directly below center of nuclear bomb blast.
ikor: in Gr. myth, the ethereal fluid flowing instead of blood
in the veins of the gods.

Manes: ancient Rom. religion concerned with souls of the dead.

windlestrain: dried stalk of grass, a slender or weak person or *thing.*

wilding: wild plant, esp. apple tree.

willy-nilly: whirlwind over desert, severe tropical cyclone (Australia).

It is now fall, and it is getting toward the day of my mother's death and the time of my own birth. I would know this without a calendar. Every year in the last week of October, the cranes come back. They come in early morning or late afternoon. You hear them before you see them. There are no words to say what they sound like. My bird book says "a loud rolling rattle," but that is not it. More a coo, a throaty twitter multiplied and divided by dozens, hundreds, thousands. A deeply pleasurable sound, this convulsion of wings stroking air. You hear all this—throat and wing—thrumming not so much in your ears but in your chest, and you look up, and there they are.

There they are. They fly in patterns with necks extended, but the patterns are always shifting even as you watch, the point of the V shifting in flight from front to back, the tail of the V forming a fledgling v behind. Some cranes remain outside the pattern while still flying in some obscure way with it. Sometimes they are so high they look like pepper. Sometimes you can see a pattern of a low-flying flock palimpsestically (to use a word to keep) posed against a higher group. Mostly, though, especially against the late setting sun, you can see them quite clearly and individually. They are in harmony, yet they are beyond harmony. They make harmony seem paltry. This would not be the extravaganza it is were it not for the way the

New Mexico sun casts light like a flamethrower casts flame, intently and arbitrarily. When the cranes' wings go up, the sun flares the silver tips into momentary flames that leap out like minor explosions. It is a spectacular migration. Over the course of several weeks you will see tens of thousands of them. There used to be whoopers, but now there are only the sandhill cranes. They follow the Rio Grande as they make their way south to Bosque del Apache National Wildlife Refuge and, for those who don't want to stop, beyond to Mexico.

When the cranes come, as they do each year at this time of the death and enfolding of living things, it is as if something has happened that cannot be taken away. Together and separately, they have beauty and they have shape, but what gives them meaning is the motion of the form, the form of the motion. The glint of wing, the V that creates and becomes its own obverse in a design that is also moving beyond itself. They are the words and they are the poem.

So they pass and so they stay, like the river falling and rising.

DEEP DELVE
Sunrise
and the river shrouded in fog.
Yet the poem will not rise,
is stuck here with me,
grappling for a toehold
among the rocks.

Go to the deep delve,
to the blind fathomless pit
where the sea rushes in

and the poem ventures out,
tilting the wind like a straw —
or a stone groping for light.
The poem will sink, must sink,
will drink darkness like a sponge
or a tree of coral bred to leaf-bone and marrow
seining the dregs, absolving the rest,
drop by bitter brackish drop.

The water deepens at the mouth
of the river, weaned on seawood and salt
applied like a poultice to old wounds
and griefs, fleshing out the poem.
The sun is dim and blue here,
blue-black as the abysmal void
before God spawned the world.
Before the waters gathered,
spewing out life whole, mother-naked
as the poem spawning its own true word.

ERIN CLAYTON PITNER

In my mother's notes, I find an explanation of this poem, presumably for a reading before an audience. On her 1983 calendar, which, strangely, has only a few dates marked in what would prove a momentous year, the year of the mutation, the threads of the cancer looping and catching, I note that she attended a poetry festival in Natchez on April 23–24. What she says in her notes is this: "Last year I spent a night at the Ramada Inn in Natchez and got up early enough the next morning to see the sun rise over the river. It was a troubled period in my life, and it helped me to be able to write this poem."

These simple statements sound strange to me. I cannot imagine my mother in the Ramada Inn by the Mississippi River trying to delve to the bottom of what it was that has made her so sad, seining her collection of words to keep for the poem to say it. I cannot see her getting up before dawn to go down to the river. I can see the thick brown current, its inexorable leaning toward salt. I can see the sun coming up on the water. But I cannot fit Erin Taylor into this scene. And this, I know, is my error and my affliction.

My mother thought of herself as the long-black-hair, drop-dead-gorgeous heroine-artist, the type of woman who would stand on the banks of the Mississippi for hours and maybe even jump in. In notebook after notebook, on page after page of scrawling, crossed-over, hard-won prose, this woman struggles into pulpy plenitude. She is wild; she is unrestrained; she is, as she herself puts it, "a bitch in heat." Her name is Marissa; sometimes she is a musician, sometimes a writer, sometimes a painter. She lives deep inside herself, a place she envisions as a dark and lovely grotto. She has hot sex with Miklos, a man from Czechoslovakia with a crazy wife who has to have shock treatments because she yearns for home. Erin's creations, Marissa and Miklos, are full of desire; they are insatiable: for sex, for art, for love. In one incarnation Miklos looks deep into Marissa's eyes "lighted by an indefinable sadness that piqued his interest" and says: "You won't be great; neither am I. But you will write music that will ease your heart and each work you produce will spur you on until you will be caught up in the aura of your own dream and I'll be there with you, sleeping and waking, working it out of that dark and lovely place. It will be hard but you will do it."

What a thrill, what a flutter—this married Czechoslova-
kian. He doesn't just talk to Marissa; he doesn't just have hot
sex with her; he tells her she's an *artist* (though perhaps not a
great one). To become the artist her destiny requires her to be,
Marissa must be very careful about one thing: she must keep
that madwoman wife locked up.

Were one inclined toward such fiction, one might turn the
page of Erin's messy notebook, eager to read more scrawlings
about such a man and such a woman, more words to keep
thrown about wildly, like Marissa and Miklos pitching their
clothes when they're trying to get naked fast. Reading Erin's
draftings of lust and beauty and art—writings she must have
had in mind when she bought her plantation desk with the
lock—one might indeed feel deliciously like a Peeping Tom.
Turning these torrid pages with a heightened pulse, however,
leads to a dissatisfying dead end. Marissa and Miklos, art and
passion, dissolve. There are several pages of white space in the
notebook, then a list of what Erin Taylor must do over the next
two mundane days:

Mon.
1. Dentist
2. Book Store—Pictures?
3. Beauty Shop
4.

Tues.
1. Family Portrait
2. Deliver gifts
3. Gas
4. Pictures

5. Allergy Shot
6. Get story off again.

I read this list, like so many I've written in my own note-books, and wonder what Erin had in mind for the vacant space after the Number 4 on Monday, after she had gotten her hair done. Was she planning to take more pills, run off the road, meet Miklos at the Natchez Trace Inn out on West Main? Or perhaps, more radically, read the dictionary and steal more words to keep?

opprobrious: abusive, disrespectful.
opprobrium: disgrace or infamy attached to conduct viewed as grossly shameful. 2. anything bringing shame or disgrace. 3. reproachful contempt for something regarded as inferior.

I returned to college to read poems the same year my mother went back to write them. I'm not sure how much we learned from our classes; it was more a matter of giving ourselves permission. Nor am I certain who went first.

"How can you leave that baby?" She is referring to my six-year-old daughter. "When are you going to find time to look after the house and do the cooking? Children need their mothers. You should wait."

I sigh. I've been working the police beat for the local newspaper at night and doing free-lance work at home during the day. I'm training "the baby" to sleep late.

I take a few English courses and then apply for a graduate teaching assistantship. "Are you married?" the acting director of the graduate program asks. "Do you have children?" he asks, looking a bit to the left of my eyes as he asks his breathy questions. He tells me I can be an intern the following year. This means that I can do everything a graduate teaching assistant does except for free, and pay my own tuition.

"It's a good thing," my mother says. "Not so much time away from the home. You know children are the most important thing, and husbands: they work hard, they expect some consideration."

Later, after I finish my M.A. and decide to get the Ph.D. and my mother asks me why I could possibly want to do such a thing, I tell her I am hoping to get a university teaching position, and my husband is going to quit his job and find work wherever we end up. She is deeply shocked by this news. "You mean he is going to give up that good job?" she asks querulously. "Why can't you teach there where you got your degree? Part-time is nice. Not so much responsibility. More time for other things. You drive yourself too hard, Minrose, and you are going to pay for it one of these days."

This too is strange, coming as it does (I did not know it then) from a woman who, around the same time we are having this conversation, is imagining herself as Christ, as Jesus in the grave. Who is this woman who can dream up such a thing for herself—that she is the son of God, the *dead* son of God in his *tomb*—but not allow her daughter the morsel of imagining herself a university professor? A draft, marked "this," written on the back of a brown paper towel for drying one's hands in a public bathroom:

It is quiet here.
The babel of voices has faded away.
The clap-trap of the hammers,
the tsk, tsk of the crowd,

the sobs of the women
are buried beneath the weight of stone.

To replenish the seed of Adam

I lie here like rotting fruit
taking on the putrid flesh of death
and all the earthswarm of humankind,
the whole stinking mass of sin and shame
to prove the certainty of the godhead
groaning for release within me.

Dawn has not yet arisen
The shadows still
hold me in their sway
of light and darkness,
Death and eternity
warring within me.
Am I real?

Am I real? The Sunday night before my weeklong prelim-
inary examinations are scheduled to begin, I am staying up late
to go over my notes one last time. I am sitting at my card table
with piles of books and notes in stacks by literary period. The
ashtray in front of me is spilling over with butts. I am queasy
from eyestrain and too many Girl Scout cookies. I am, through
unfortunate timing, this year's block captain for the cookie
drive, and empty boxes of Thin Mints are strewn all over the
floor. I have kept a running tally of what I owe my daughter's
troop.

Thin Mints: 9 boxes
Samoas: 8 boxes

Do-si-dos: 6 boxes
Tagalongs: 3 boxes
TOTAL SO FAR: 26 boxes

When the phone rings, it is past midnight. My heart, already skittish, seizes convulsively as I scramble to answer before it can ring a second time and wake up everyone in the house. I fear that someone has run off the road one time too many.

Before I can say hello, my mother whispers over the line, "Minrose, I can't stand it any longer. I'm going to leave him. This time I mean it. I'm afraid of what he is going to do."

"What's happened now." I am thinking just how profoundly tired I am. How crowded my brain is with all these damn dates and periods and millions upon millions of words, words, words. I am sick to death of words.

"Minrose, this is it. No more. I refuse to live under these conditions. He locks himself down in the basement. He eats at the Holiday Inn. He won't talk to me."

"He's never talked to you before. Mama, I'm studying for my exams. They start tomorrow."

"I don't care what you're doing, Minrose. It's always something. I want you to come down here and get me out of this house. Now. Tomorrow morning. There are things I'm not telling you. Things you wouldn't believe."

"Mama, you know I can't just drop everything right now. You've been married to him for almost thirty years. You can wait one week."

"Minrose, you will be responsible for what happens if I have to wait. It will be me who pays the price. As usual. You always were the selfish one. He won't say a single word to me. Not a word."

She hangs up before I can say anything else. I light another cigarette, expecting the phone to ring again. It does not.

Today I read in the paper that, even in the new millennium, older women in China, especially those from the villages, still suffer from bound feet. Their poor feet look like tiny fists, the small toes broken and forced by the binding to turn inward under the foot, making the large toe appear grotesquely rotund. It was usually the mother who would bind her young daughter's feet; then the little girl would hobble painfully from chore to chore. (In those days a man did not care whether a girl was pretty, one old woman said; he just looked at the feet. He just wanted those baby feet.) Once a week or so the mother would loosen the bindings to wash her daughter's feet. This would hurt more than the binding itself. Afterward the girl would not be able to walk for several days.

In my mother's snowdrift notebook I find on a back page the remnant of a scribbled, much-crossed-over poem, a poem I have never seen before:

> His name is legion —
> a thousand demons unleashed
> like swine wallowing in the
> pitmire of rage and fear.
> He is a turncoat
> a switchblade at the throat.
> Love gnawing its own entrails.
> He is the small print

in the marriage decree
she never bothered to read
on that fateful day.
She is the hag-ridden shrew
behind the curtains tightly drawn
to hide her wounds.

She is the hairline crack
of the fractured brow
when the headache is too
intense to bear.

And another untitled fragment:

A woman searching for a way out, scrabbling
at the lock of the door. The air is fetid here,
fouled with blood and entrails where millions
have lived and died, imprisoned by their own flesh.

And scribbled on the last page of the notebook, this:

the mind ticks on like a time bomb
waiting for the poem to free her.

In my mother's dusty boxes the biggest surprise of all is a small
yellow form, which has been torn out of a spiral notebook, a
traffic citation and accident report written by Officer R. L.
Johnson of the Mississippi Highway Patrol. What it says is
this:

In a blue 1976 Oldsmobile, Erin T. Pitner was driving west
on Mississippi Highway 6 right outside of Oxford when, at
4:50 P.M., the Olds suddenly veered into the oncoming lane,

sideswiping the oncoming car of a twenty-three-year-old man from North Carolina and forcing him off the road. Both cars were damaged. Erin T. was cited for driving on the wrong side of the road. (She was examined at The Surgical Clinic at Oxford at a cost of thirty-five dollars and, a week after the accident, paid the justice of the peace forty-three dollars on the citation. There is no record of whether the man in the other car was hurt.)

None of this information shocks me. I knew my mother's penchant was for running off the road, though I had thought she stayed on her own side of it, not endangering the rest of the world by trying her hand at head-on collisions. But the surprise lies not in the event itself but in the date on the traffic ticket: July 1, 1981. This is Erin T.'s birthday. Her sixtieth.

So let me stop now, let me imagine this woman. Today she is sixty years old. She is driving to Oxford on Highway 6. Perhaps to an evening class. Perhaps she looks down at the notebook on the seat beside her, the white notebook with a snowdrift on the front. Last year's notebook of words to keep, and letters of the alphabet to tuck them into. She is thinking of a word. Perhaps a word like

dehiscence: 1. the natural bursting open of capsules, fruits, anthers, etc., for the discharge of their contents. 2. Biol. the release of materials by the splitting open of an organ or tissue.

She knows she will lose *dehiscence* forever if she doesn't find the *D* page in her snowdrift notebook and write it in. She leans over to find a pen in her purse, her hand loosening on the steering wheel, and, oh, the car, and oh, and oh.

❈ ❈ ❈

Now the Erin in my office opens one eye.

Dehiscence. Yes. There was something about that day. The sun was in my eyes and it was too hot to draw breath. The air was like a swamp. Yes, everything was splitting and cracking. Everything was coming apart. I was thinking that the line in the middle was the split. I was thinking I needed to get to the other side.

Now she sits up from her nap and pulls the net off her hair, which remains plastered to her head.

I was thinking about you too. The husband, nice man, he'd talk and laugh. He was always telling you how smart you were, smarter than he was, he would say, and just one baby and not alone with it, not stuck with it all by yourself, not the three of them eating you up alive, taking it all so that when you were sixty you wouldn't have anything left over. You didn't have to fix a meal. You would read all day if you wanted to and open a can of spaghetti sauce at night. Or say, let's go out, and everyone would say, sure, that's a good idea, and maybe a movie too. I fed you my dreams and you ate them up. All of you just ate them right up in five minutes, like at supper when I'd just be getting my breath to eat and you all would be through and ready to move on, leaving me there with the dishes in that hot kitchen after I shelled all those peas and fried the okra in that heat. You ate your fill and didn't think one minute about popping back out to play red rover and catch lightning bugs, and then I'd be left at the table eyeing those peas congealing in the bowl. One night I sat there and stared at them for hours until finally it got dark outside and I turned on the radio.

"Your mother was jealous of you." I meet an old friend of my mother at a women's studies conference. We have lunch in the cafeteria. This old friend of my mother is three years older than I am. I was jealous of how my mother loved her. So was the salesman. She leans over the table. "Your mother was jealous of you," she says for the second time, tapping her fingernail on the table. "She wanted your life. She wanted to be you."

Dear Minrose,
I wanted to be free like you are but I just can't get past that writer's block.

In the last five years of her life, my mother changed her will at least a dozen times. She would write me long incoherent letters about how her wedding ring was now going to go to my sister because I had not been to see her recently. Or my grandmother's scholarship pin would go to my sister's daughter instead of my daughter because I had been the one to lock Mama up.

At one point she became furious with my brother, who had not written her a thank-you note for a meal she had served him, and cut him out entirely. One such letter contained a list of all our sins and pronounced that she hoped we died first, but if we didn't she was leaving everything to my daughter, but only if and when she married.

In the extant will, Erin Taylor commands me to edit and publish her poetry into a book.

ARTICLE XI

Upon my death, my filing cabinet containing all of my writings is to be immediately locked and the keys shall be given to my daughter, Minrose Bryan Gwin, whom I designate to take charge of all of my writings, both published and unpublished. I direct that my Executor set aside a sufficient sum of money from the residue of my estate which shall be used by my daughter, Minrose Bryan Gwin, to edit and publish a book of my writings; said funds shall be set aside before any division of the residual estate is made and shall not exceed $2,500.00. Any proceeds derived from the sale of such book and other published writings shall be delivered to my Executor and made a part of my estate, after Minrose Bryan Gwin shall have reimbursed herself for any expenses not paid for out of the funds set forth herein above. Further, in the event that Minrose Bryan Gwin shall require assistance in the editing of said book, she is hereby directed to hire such an assistant and said book should contain the following language:

"For my Mother and Father" . . .

Said book shall also contain the following language after the title: "By Erin Clayton Pitner, as edited by her daughter, Minrose Bryan Gwin."

If feasible, a short forward should be written by Minrose Bryan Gwin.

This is not the book my mother wanted. On the computer screen my words seem etched in fire. I look at what I have written, the papers piled on my desk with Erin's words and mine. From a distance they are indistinguishable. Drafts of drafts. Stories of stories. I would not be surprised to see them burst into flame. Spontaneous combustion.

After my mother died, there was no money, and the salesman kept her papers so that I didn't receive them until his death a decade later. But in the summer of 1993, I got together all of Erin's poems I could find, wrote for permissions, filed for copyright, and published a book of her poems with her chosen title: *Stones and Roses.* There is a charcoal sketch of an abstract spiral on the cover. It was drawn by an art student who took several of my feminist theory classes and who, for reasons she never would explain, limited herself to black and white and shades between. The spiral sketch was so abstract the layout designer at first put it upside down on the mock-up design of the cover. I arranged the poems from the information I had and wrote a short introduction. The representative from the printing company I chose to produce Erin's book said the company could print five hundred copies for almost the same amount as one hundred. So I ordered five hundred.

When I received the shipment of Erin's books, contained in four large cardboard boxes, I began to send them to family members, friends, and libraries. I placed them in several bookstores. That left me with about 440 books, which I did not know what to do with.

Should I send them to a women's prison, I asked myself. No, because they would incite riots. Should I send them to public school libraries in Mississippi as the work of a state poet? No, they might cause mass suicides among the youth of the land. At one point I stole a hometown phone book from a phone booth so that I could mark off people I could send the book to. In the middle of doing so, I froze, picturing myself on the closet floor, feeling at home there with the familiar names, the smell of shoe leather, perhaps even a jar of sweet pickles. So Erin's books, laid neatly back to back in their boxes, remained stored, under wraps, unread. I locked them up in my office at school, just to get them out of the house because they posed a fire hazard.

The Erin in my office pokes her finger through the hairnet

she's been holding in her hand. Then she starts tearing little
bits of it apart.

*Why didn't you just set up a stand and sell them in the street like
cantaloupes? You never did really put yourself out unless it came to locking me up. I would have changed the will but things got confused. The
lawyer said I had already changed it too many times. Then he stopped
answering my phone calls.*

Dear Mother of the Will:
Guess what. I don't have to do what you say anymore because you are dead.

Sincerely,
Your Living Daughter

FIRST BOOK
Five years and 41 poems
typed and retyped, quaking
on the page like jello pudding
half-cooked, or Santa's belly
belted down for the wild impetuous
trip. Ashes, switches and soot signing
my forehead like a pilgrim on a perilous
journey of words, trapped midway between
heaven and ashpit.

1,825 days of work squeezed from
every niche and cranny of the house
heaped with dirt swept beneath dusty carpets
where poems sprout like mushrooms shattering
at my touch, when the vacuum roars down upon
them like a firestorm gobbling them up.

41 poems refusing to fall
into place like kids chasing
fireflies just beyond their reach
or toddlers with fragile fingers
clutching at the moon.

Half-naked poems peering
back at me, impertinent, unafraid.
Heartbread of my life spread wantonly
upon the page.

ERIN CLAYTON PITNER

When my mother was let out of the first mental hospital in seven weeks flat, the first thing she did was call me to gloat. "I suppose you thought you were rid of me, Minrose. Well here I am right back and I am just fine. The doctors think I am just fine. All I needed was a rest, they say, and proper diet and medication. I have gained weight and I am just as sane as you are and don't you forget it, young lady, because I'm home to stay." Before I could respond, she hung up.

I put down the phone and sank to the kitchen floor. I sat there very still for over an hour. My husband still had a sore place on his shin where she had kicked him when he helped pick her up and take her to the hospital. "Admit it," he said later. "Every one of us loved it. We loved having her in our control for just that one moment when we could do it and it was all right just that once." There was still a scab on my chest where she had nicked me with the scissors.

The next day she called back. "Come see me," she said as if she hadn't talked to me the day before. "I'm home from the hospital and I feel good."

It is April and everything in Mississippi is blooming to beat the band when I drive down from Virginia. I am coming for a class reunion. After that I will see my mother. The old girl-friends rent some rooms in a motel one night and sit up and talk. We are lying around on two double beds telling about our lives, or so we say. We pass pictures of our children if we have children.

One friend doesn't say anything. We ask her about her life. She says the past year wasn't so good. She just went to bed and couldn't seem to get up. She does not know why. She quit her job. Then someone had to be brought in to take care of her children and do the housework. One of the girlfriends says, "I guess we all have times like that." We all nod vigorously. There is a long silence. Then someone says, "Let's play bridge like we used to."

The next morning I ask an old friend to ride with me to my mother's house. This is the same friend whose car I wrecked when I was fourteen. She was teaching me to drive and before we'd gotten a full block, I saw an upcoming curve, hit the accelerator instead of the brake, and slammed into a parked car. Before the police came, I begged her to switch places with me. We switched, and she told everyone she had been driving and never told her parents otherwise. She knew they would call mine and my mother and the salesman would kill me. Now she waits outside in the car with instructions to call the police if I do not reappear in fifteen minutes. She has known my mother for twenty years. She does not ask questions. I can tell she is relieved that I haven't asked her to come into the house with me.

I need not have been afraid. Erin Taylor is still on her medicine from the mental hospital (this will not last) and is by far the most pleasant she has ever been since I've known her. Her voice has one speed and one tone. She says: "How are you. How is the family. How is the dog. Oh how nice you look. You do look wonderful. Yes I am fine."

She loves seeing me and she has a secret to show me. She wants me to come back to her room down the long dark hall. I am careful. I drop back to walk behind her. When she reaches the door to her room, she turns and smiles at me, narrowing her eyes like a flirty girl leading her lover to bed. The thought crosses my mind that she's been mistakenly lobotomized. Her stockings, I notice, still droop and bloom at her ankles. She has a handful of torn Kleenexes, which, as she turns, she tosses in the air as if to anoint the moment. "I picked them all," she says, without prefix, "all of them. The whole yard I picked for you. *Look.*"

Slowly she opens the door. I peer inside, dubious. The floor of her room is covered in spring flowers. It is April in Mississippi and my mother has a garden in her room. Strands of forsythia bow from corners onto a carpet of white clematis bruised and wilted, sweet beyond anything you could dream. The scent makes me woozy. Jonquils, yellow bells my mother calls them, droop from toppled vases. When I leave, she gives me some sprigs of clematis to take home. There is nothing that smells as sweet as clematis, and I distinctly remember how the car was full of the smell of it from just a few sprigs I put in a paper cup on the seat. Later I will know that this was the last day, the last good time. I will write a poem about my druggy mother and her garden room, how she loved me that one day and how I drove fourteen hours home in a trance, drunk on sweet motherlove. It is later still, years later, when I will realize suddenly that her clematis never bloomed before July and usually not until August. It never bloomed in the spring.

What is dreaming but memory's long flight south? Spring and my mother with clematis trailing behind her, like the bride with me her jittery groom. It is too soon, I say, clematis doesn't bloom in April, I say. It did this year, she sings. For you it bloomed early. This year it bloomed early for you.

Clematis, my cousin tells me, can bloom more than once a season, sometimes in early spring and late summer too. Sometimes when least expected.

The mother of the woman who steals my card table every spring has come to visit. The two of them are cooking together in the kitchen. This mother, long-boned and Irish, cooked for eight children. They all lived in one side of a shotgun house near the industrial canal in New Orleans's Ninth Ward. Their father would plunk them into the backseat of the old car, which he had stuffed with Spanish moss to fill in the holes in the seat covers, and take them to City Park to feed the ducks, driving all the way in third gear. This mother made stuffed artichokes, meatless spaghetti sauce with eggs floating on the top, milk-heavy French toast with cinnamon. Once when she was visiting and I made a colorful pasta salad, she applauded when I brought it to the table.

Before I committed my mother the first time, I came into her kitchen to find four pots busily boiling away on the stove. When I lifted the lids, I found canned green beans in all four of them. I opened the kitchen cabinet. Inside were rows and rows of nothing but green beans. When I asked Mama why she was eating nothing but green beans when she weighed less than eighty pounds, she told me to mind my own business, that she liked green beans and besides she was a grown woman and could eat whatever she wanted.

By the time of her second commitment, she had gotten tired of green beans and had begun to eat nothing but hamburger meat and bread and butter sweet pickles. She had gained thirty pounds and the roaches were having a field day. There were opened, half-consumed sweet pickle jars stashed in the bottom of closets and under beds throughout the house. The hamburger meat, all of it raw, was a more serious problem. By this time she had not only begun to eat off the floor but also to believe that she was cooking off of it. When I came into the house after the deputies had taken her out, the smell made me gasp. There was rotten meat spilling out of cooking pots on the floor, formed into patties and left on plates on the floor, piled up in the refrigerator and freezer and in kitchen cabinets next to the dishes. There were huge moldy mounds of it under the kitchen sink where the garbage can had once been. To the right of the mounds were bottles of sherry and gin shiny with grease.

When I began to look for my first academic job, I decided I needed to lose weight. (I then weighed 125 pounds at five feet five inches tall.) I began to eat baked potatoes because I liked them and they filled me up. I discovered that I liked them more and more. I generally ate one for lunch and then ate one with beef or chicken for dinner. "Mama," my daughter would complain, "I'm tired of baked potatoes. Let's have macaroni. Let's have rice." I began to fix my husband and daughter their regular meals and myself a baked potato. I found that at dinner the potato filled me up just fine and I didn't need anything else. I began to bake my potatoes seven or eight at a time. I was losing weight and saving time and getting job interviews. I would lie in bed at night with my hands on my hips, pressing for the bone. When I would shower, my hair would wash down and stop up the drain. I felt both tired and oddly exhilarated.

I do not know when I stopped eating baked potatoes. It did not happen all at once. I do not remember whether it was before or after I got my first job. What I remember are the pots appearing on the top of the stove (from whose hand? my husband's? my daughter's? my own?), how good they began to smell, how I began to want spicy sauces and hearty stews, how I bought new cookbooks and developed for the first time in my life a desire to make jellies and preserves, pickles sweet and sour.

COMPLAINT

Always the same.
Manna.
Heavenly flakes of bread
dew-fresh each day
only to gather.

The blandness of bread
they sighed,
yearning for seeds
in gritty hands,
the coarseness of grain
between the teeth,
stone ground.

ERIN CLAYTON PITNER

❀ ❀ ❀

Now I sit across the table from Ruth and her mother, Zenobia, and see their cheekbones rise up in their faces at the exact
same angle. Their fingers move through the air in the same patterns. They make sentences into questions with the same in-
flections. (Since they do not do this except with each other, I
assume it is because they want to please each other especially.)
When they are happy, which they are in each other's presence,
their dark eyes gleam like the two lighted candles between
them.

My daughter Carol does not look like me, but there is
something about her mouth that is mine. She laughs and people will say you laugh just like your mother. She moves
her hand before her face and I see the shadow of my own
gesture. Our hands are all alike: my grandmother's, my
mother's, mine, my daughter's. They are small and fleshy.
Our fingers are short. Our fingernails are small and brittle.
They chip and tear; we could not grow them long if our lives
depended on doing so. (Once, at an airport, a woman sitting
next to me waiting for a plane took one of my hands and
said: "I am a nurse, and your fingernails look strange. The
nails can be a sign of serious illness. You should see a doctor." After that, I began looking at my hands for signs;
though I do not know what I am looking for, I continue to
look. Increasingly I see enlarged veins, spots, and strange
swellings, and I know what they mean.) These hands of ours
are for holding pencils and cigarettes, turning the pages of
books, cooking some food and cleaning up after a sick baby
or dog or horse, pulling on the reins or flinging out the
words. They are not for show, and they are not for making or
fixing small things.

The one dress my mother made me took her weeks though it was the simplest pattern she could find. The first day I wore it to school, I raised my right arm during my first-period class and the right underarm seam split. At lunchtime I reached for my milk in the cafeteria and the left underarm seam split. By the end of the day, half the hem was out and the up and down seams on either side of the dress had gaps in them. When I came home in my failing dress and my mother saw what had happened, her shoulders began to jerk up and down. She grabbed the bottom of the dress and tried to pull it off over my head. It caught me on the neck and I thought she was going to choke me to death pulling it over my head, but she finally got it off and started swatting me over the head with it. *"I told you to be careful now you've gone and ruined it ruined it and here I spent hours and hours and hours trying to make you something nice."* Then she tore what was left of it into pieces and threw them in the garbage. The next day she took the borrowed sewing machine back to her brother's wife, who made all of her girls' matching outfits. She never sewed me anything again except for her famous bedroom slippers.

Years later, Mama decided she'd take another crack at sewing and got another sewing machine, a castoff from someone. She had finally found something she could make. It was a pattern in *McCall's* for bedroom slippers. You take two new matching washcloths and sew them together on three of the four sides. Then you turn down a hem of about an inch on the loose outside of each washcloth and sew it up. You get yourself a large safety pin and some elastic. You cut the elastic about sixteen inches long and lead it through the sewed-up hem with the safety pin. Then you tie the elastic tight but not too tight. (Remove the safety pin first!) For people with big feet, you get large wash clothes and allow more play in the elastic; for children and women with little feet, like Erin and me, you get small ones and make the elastic tighter. You try to get the cloths thick but not so thick that it's hard to sew them up. There is one more step, and it is fun. You sew a jingle bell on each of the toe ends. Now you have some nice fluffy bedroom slippers that make whoever wears them look like an elf.

My mother was thrilled with herself for learning how to sew the slippers, and over a period of twenty or so years she made hundreds of them. (She made me at least two dozen pair.) They were the perfect gift, she would say. They were cheap, and they wore out so that you could make a person another pair at least every other year. (Erin Taylor kept charts and graphs of people and years and sizes so she'd know whose slippers were wearing out and when she needed to save the day.) Moreover, they were highly individual; you varied the fabric, the color, the placement of the jingle bells so that each time you gave someone another pair, they felt and looked brand new.

My grandmother got a manicure at the beauty shop every week of her conscious adult life. She liked to sit under the dryer and hold her fingertips in a bowl of warm water to soften the cuticles. She was always too warm under the dryer (and elsewhere) and would wipe her face with a lace handkerchief and fan herself with a pleated fan made in Japan, which she held in one hand while the beauty shop manicurist polished the nails of the other with "Dusty Rose," worn also by her sister (Jane Stuart of the Milk of Magnesia, the southern belle sister who had the good sense not to shoot herself, or die in child-birth, or become a lesbian college president). When she had to wash the supper dishes, she would start the water in the kitchen sink in a trickle and rub the rims of cups and surface of dishes with her pink-tipped fingers under the running water, careful not to chip or tear her tiny nails.

My daughter bites her nails and the fleshy cuticle around them. She controls twelve-hundred-pound horses with her ragged hands. Last year she made a New Year's resolution to quit chewing herself to bits, but her poor fingertips are still raw and cracked, puffed over their tiny slices of nails.

When my mother would be thinking hard about something, she would nibble the nail on her right index finger. As I sit at my computer I see reflected in the screen's glare a woman doing the same thing.

In Erin's snowdrift notebook, there is an unfinished poem that describes a photograph of my grandmother taken when she was sixteen. The portrait is a side view. Minrose's hair is thick and dark and piled atop her head, which seems, under its mass of coils, too ponderous for the stalk-like neck. Min-rose the girl is looking down, her mouth curved in a slight smile, as if she is contemplating something good to eat. There are pages of Erin's scribbled, scratched-out lines. She struggles to capture her mother's reflection. The poem never settles, except for the first line: "And there you are."

And there you are:
Black hair tucked up . . .

And there you are:
in a gilded frame . . .

And there you are:
Framed by velvet and lace . . .

And there you are.

I am taking my mother to the National Gallery in Washington, D.C. She has a coffee-table picture book of art called *The Century of Impressionists*. Unlike most people, she really reads her coffee-table art book and worries over the pictures like someone studying for a test. She has never been to the National Gallery. She went to New York on her honeymoon with the salesman, but she never went to any galleries there either. She has all her life wanted to visit Paris and the Louvre. She has never been to Europe. She is excited. She is walking fast from room to room. She is looking for the French Impressionists. She wants to find Mary Cassatt.

When we get to the exhibit rooms for Impressionists, her exclamations become louder and louder. "Just look. Look at that one. Oh my. Ooh. I can't believe I'm seeing this. And *this*. Look, look, Minrose, *look*." People are staring at us. I walk to the other side of the room, trying to elude her. Perhaps if she doesn't have me to exclaim to she will quiet down.

Suddenly she turns and sees on the back wall Renoir's *Girl with Watering Can*. She stops in her tracks and bursts into loud sobs in front of the painting. "I've waited all my life to see you," she cries out to the painting, flinging wide her arms, "and there you are! *There you are*."

How far can the shade, the shape, of something you have not yet imagined take you? The curved hand that makes the weight of the can visible. The way the burden becomes pleasurable if hefted just so, and often. Erin knows that beauty is

strong enough to plunder the eye, the heart. It is beauty that
is the burden.

VAN GOGH

Think of it.
Imagine this.
The flow from head to heart to hand.
The glory in the handheld heartbeat
of poem to palette.

Peach blossoms aswirl with light,
shells of pink-petaled light humming.

The sea unfurling in his hand
laving dark strands of earth
streaked with saffron.

And sunflowers reseeding themselves
each more frenzied than the other.

Blue too, blaring above raw gold wheat
writhing toward the bruised rim
of the horizon
raucous with crows
swarming over the burnished breadth
of the passion.

ERIN CLAYTON PITNER

My mother, creator of those two wild lovers Marissa and Miklos, never said the word *passion* in my presence. In the girls'
bathroom Madeline Ives tells me to go fuck myself. I am in the
sixth grade and I ask Madeline, who is not a nice girl, what

"fuck" means. "You're kidding," she says. "You don't know *that?*" She points her middle finger on her left hand and makes a circle with her thumb and forefinger with her right. She inserts the former into the latter. "He sticks *his* you-know into *her* hole," she says with enormous satisfaction. For years I consider this act so distasteful that I envision it being accomplished over the toilet, perhaps the effect of having been told it while surrounded by toilets. I see a male sitting on the toilet with a female sitting in his lap. I see a female on the toilet with a male kneeling before her. I wonder how long it takes.

Once my mother began in a halting way to try to tell me something about sex. She broached the topic so obscurely that it took me a while to figure out what she was talking about. I was seventeen by then and knew much more than she thought I did. "Oh Mama," I said, "that's okay. I know about all that." She looked shocked, then angry. She put her hands on her hips and said, "Well, young lady, you don't know *nearly* as much as you think you do." Then she turned and strode from the room. A few minutes later she came back and stood in the doorway, her apron gathered like an offering in clenched fists. "It's not what you think," she said, looking down at her hands as if surprised by them. "It's never what you think."

NIGHT SONG

A winter night of storm.
The low fire, crimson, crooning
the ancient tuneless song
of the circle tightly drawn.

Well-bred, the silent cat hugs
her home and hearth.

She sleeps serene, well-fed,
dreaming little, caring less.

Yet even now she is stirring
in her sleep,
turning, softly moaning,
crying out
she leaps toward door
and darkness,
vacillates, leaning to the fire
she waits.

She feels what I cannot hear
and dare not feel.

Flinging off hand and home
she springs into the night
and is quickly gone, seeking
the destined darkness
of the vast and lovely storm.

ERIN CLAYTON PITNER

After my mother began to take writing workshops, she would write me letters about how passion abrades form, though that was not how she put it. It seemed to me, reading these letters, that Erin's problem was always the problem of form. Nothing she ever did fit precisely the thing it was supposed to fit; this curious imprecision gave her poems a lovely edginess that, like the cranes on their flights south, moved in and out of what was intended. There was sometimes beauty, and perhaps pleasure too, in such lapses of calibration when form collapsed and gathered itself anew.

Dear Minrose,
In my class I am reading sonnets and having to write them.
The professor thinks it is important for us to learn to write
within the forms. These forms. They don't fit if you know
what I mean.

Love,
Mama

COSMOGRAPH

Little man, spare me small verities dubbed
and dumped inchoate into the poem
without a wrinkle or a ridge, a dome
of dogma bolstering words mortared
each by side seamless, marbleized.
Lines mitered without a query to roam
and wriggle free, formless as a dream
to float tender, chancy, unguarded.

O small man, with rule and stylus to chart earth
roiling in space, spun-struck with stars, gold-flung
by moons welling with celestia before flesh
was begotten—while she strums the wind,
Woman brooding galactea, full-wrought,
Maggie Muse, increscent, burgeoning.

ERIN CLAYTON PITNER

Today I feel Erin may rise from her bed in my office, walk right
through the door I have kept closed since beginning to work
on this book, and come into the living room for a visit. I will
look up and say, oh hello, Mama. I have been expecting you.
This is Ruth. This is her mother, Zenobia, who is also visiting.

Isn't it nice you two could be here at the same time. Let me give you some posole. Let me take your suitcase. Let me put my hands on your poor swollen belly so that I can know you are really you.

After she got over my daughter's too-soon birth, my mother was a pleasant houseguest the few times she visited me. She did not scream at me or criticize the way I did things. She liked my crippled dog, and they took long slow walks, my mother pacing herself to the dog's hobbled gait. I lived for several years on the edge of a forest that had many paths going through it. She would go out with the dog in the morning and not return until early afternoon. When she visited in the fall, she would gather leaves. The woods were full of dogwood, redbud, poplar, oak, and maple. She would bring in what she considered the most perfect leaves from each kind of tree and paste them into scrapbooks as my daughter had done when she was a little girl. In the spring she would gather the mayapple blossoms, always hidden like tiny church bells, she would say, under their deep green leaves in the darkest part of the woods. It was as if she were taking a vacation from herself.

When my brother or sister would run away from home, sometimes one or the other would end up at my place in Tennessee tired, smelly, and broke, having hitchhiked north. When they had had a few days to recover, they would call home and my mother would come up to get them. She would come chastened by their rebellion and everyone would have a good time together at my house. It would be like a regular family for a few days. The television or radio would be playing. My daughter's friends would be running in and out, and the dogs would be tracking in mud. There would be coffee and talk. Sometimes it would make me feel so good to see them like that, I would bake cookies just to make it better. Then they would go back home and the trouble would start back up. My mother storming up and down the hall, slapping and slamming and screaming. My brother and sister locking themselves in their rooms or running away to their friends. The salesman sleeping down in his office in the basement or staying on the road. I didn't actually know what went on in the house after I left. I knew my brother had become completely silent and my sister was failing school. I knew both thought I had abandoned them, which I had.

Over the past decade, my sister, who lives right outside of our hometown, has called me a total of about four or five times. She calls when it snows. "Hey there," she will say, her drawl raspy from years of smoking and hollering on the factory assembly line. "Guess what."

"It's snowing," I'll say.

"How'd you know?" she will answer. "We're having a dadgum blizzard here. I've never seen anything like it!"

"That's great," I'll say. "Anything else going on?"

"Nope, that's about it. I think I'm going to get me a sled."

"That sounds like the thing to do," I'll say. "Good to hear from you."

This summer my sister came to see me for the first time. She stayed six nights. We didn't talk much, but we would sit out in the backyard under the moon and stars while she would smoke. One day at lunch I made egg and olive sandwiches. She didn't remember that Mama liked them, and she didn't much like them herself. Being in the Southwest, she sensibly wanted tamales and enchiladas and green chile. Once or twice as we would sit under the big sky at night, I would say something about how Mama liked this or Mama did that. My sister would nod, at least I think she did. I'd be peering through the dark to make out her face, looking for the bone, the curve of jaw or eye socket that would seem familiar, homelike. She wondered where to get the best deals on earrings and marveled at the lack of mosquitoes.

The house my mother lived in during the last twenty or so years of her life had been built on a beautiful rolling lot with a huge oak tree to the side of it. The house was a nice shade of gray with white shutters. It had a wholesome red brick chimney on the front and a screened porch on the side. It looked like the all-American house. It was completed the year I went off to college, the salesman having had a few flush years before the silver crash, when he lost most of what he had. He was always losing and gaining, and I think he liked it that way. Perhaps it reminded him of seeing those lights on the aircraft carriers come up suddenly and knowing he had only one shot at a landing. I remember feeling jealous that my brother and sister were going to get to grow up in a nice house that wasn't rental property.

Despite its benign façade and despite the fact that it was new, over the years I came to think, irrationally to be sure, that the house itself was evil, with its long hall and strange juxtaposition of rooms so that you couldn't see from one into the other. You were always turning sharp corners and being confronted with something or someone you didn't know was there. At times I thought that there might be something *scientifically* wrong with the house and lot, something like negative energy particles or bad water or toxicity from insecticides. If my mother could just escape those particles (natural or supernatural) or stop drinking the water, then she would live happily ever after and we would all be safe.

I can feel trouble in a place. When I moved with my husband and daughter to Virginia, a real estate agent took us to a house out from town. It was a ramshackle but attractive place with cedar siding and several acres of trees just outside the city limits. It backed up to an old rock quarry. It looked like the perfect place, and it was priced much lower than we expected.

The minute we entered the house, I felt something. There was a clotted texture to the air. I felt I was not getting enough oxygen. The late afternoon sun's rays rode the air in an odd way, as if it were a struggle for them to make their path through the atmosphere inside. There was a feeling of engorgement, an unevenness in the air pressure, which increased as we went down the stairs to the basement room, a long dark area running the length of the house. It was about half underground, I judged, with high short windows. It was an odd place. Nothing seemed right, but I could see nothing really *wrong* either.

Then I looked up. There on the ceiling, suspended by chains, was a full-length mirror. That's all, just a full-length mirror. It was swaying ever so slightly, almost imperceptibly, back and forth. Surely explainable, but an odd thing, an out-of-place thing.

It was the mirror's being out of place that, strangely, led me to know that something had happened here in this place, perhaps in the very spot where I was standing, looking up at a woman in her thirties with a slightly harried look on her face, a woman who had a lot on her mind, a woman with enough ghosts of her own, thank you very much. As I peered above at the woman in the mirror, I felt another presence. I felt that someone was looking at me as if I myself were the mirror, as a cat will look out a window at nightfall and see both into and through its own reflection. I knew that this someone was hopeful. This someone was thinking, here is a way to get back to the golden earth; here is a reflecting pool through which to swim back.

"I don't like it," I heard myself saying.

"What?" my husband asked. He was irritated. We had been looking for a house just like this. We'd been looking for three days straight for just this house at just this price.

"I don't like it either," our daughter said. "It's too dark. I wouldn't have fun down here."

I took Carol's hand and put my hand on her shoulder.

"We hate it," I said, marching her toward the stairs, and thinking just how much I sounded like my mother.

Years later someone at a party said a crime had been committed in that house, but he didn't know what it was or why. He thought a body had been found in the rock quarry. Maybe more than one.

What happened in Erin's new house with the long hall and sharp corners was that over the course of time the house itself became infected and sickened. It was we who were the poison, and the poison got into the bloodstream. By the end of my mother's life, the house was nothing but dead. Like the troubled dead Christ of Erin's poem, though, it would come back to life. It would, like poor Jesus down there among the corpses, say "Am I real?" And rise again.

❉ ❉ ❉

I open the door. It squeaks. It is summer and I am home from my first year at the women's college up the road. I am fifteen minutes late from a date   tiptoe lightly so lightly down the long long hall.   Will I make it   lightly so lightly   the hall is so long the tile creaks.   Minrose Minrose   the light comes on blinding.   What time is it   why are you late   punish punish you'll be punished   how many times have I told you.

I open the door. It squeaks. I am pregnant but nobody knows. Think thin   lightly lightly walk so lightly. Does my mother have x-ray vision?   Can she see the one inside   get me to the bathroom I am going to throw up.

I open the door. It squeaks. Mama in the hospital with cancer and I am staying in the house by myself with the salesman. I am coming in late from the hospital   don't disturb   tiptoe tiptoe down the long dark hall. Suddenly I hear a roar like a lion then a gagging sound like someone is getting choked to death   then high-pitched voices little quacky voices like the Chipmunks on the radio calling back and forth to one another Christmas Christmas time is here time for joy and time for cheer. For sure, the salesman is killing someone in the back of the house. I turn around and run out the front door   call my brother from a pay phone. Oh Yes he says daddy locks himself up and makes those noises. He used to do it at the warehouse now he does it at home too   it's been going on for years didn't Mama tell you? I go stay with my sister in her trailer out in the country. She puts me in the extra room where the rats have made a hole under the bed. I hear them rustle in and out of the hole. I sit up all night in the bed and bounce to keep the rats from coming through.

I open the door. It squeaks. Mama Mama where are you

Mama. *I'm right around the next corner and I have the scissors. You want to take me away and I'm not going to let you. I'll kill you first.*

I open the door. It squeaks. No one is here now. I am alone in the house. She is in the psych ward of the local hospital. The salesman has flown the coop. No one here but me. That smell. Open the refrigerator   spoiled hamburger meat pounds and pounds of it. In the cabinet nothing but cans of green beans nothing but thousands no millions of green beans   under the sink the garbage can missing   garbage piled up where the can used to be   you used to be a good housekeeper at least   odd pieces of cut material all over the sofa and scattered down the hall like Hansel and Gretel   down the long long hall I tiptoe lightly lightly following the trail   in your room on the floor skillets pots and pans knives forks   brass candelabra a family heirloom   tampons used and unused   for what?   a china figurine of Alice in Wonderland reading a book   more spoiled hamburger sealed in Tupperware   unopened Christmas presents   a silver bowl twenty-fifth wedding anniversary gift from the three of us children I picked it out   more pieces of cut material and cut up newspaper also stored (to seal in freshness?) in Tupperware   dirty clothes   sanitary pads   the blood-red enema bag let's not forget that   how can anyone clean this up   I'm going to have to get some help. But how to explain   telephone books with pages cut out   part of a birthday cake hard as a rock *Happy* still visible   cards and letters Dear Tatie hope you're feeling better   thought this card would cheer you up   *If ever you're feeling blue just know there are lots of us making wishes for a happier you*   Love, Frances   envelopes addressed to friends and family   under the greasy stained sheets neat piles of clean clothing   underwear stockings slacks blouses dresses towels   tucked under the gray pillow   old photographs yellow and frayed at the edges   Erin Taylor a little girl with sunhat   she squints at the sun in front of the stronger-than-a-tornado house   she holds up a flower and she is happy she is smiling   under the same pillow   emery boards Vaseline   an ice pick   an ice pick?

There is such a thing as crazy-mother bonding. This can occur unexpectedly any time two women who have crazy mothers are having a conversation. It happens when one realizes the other also has had a crazy mother, and it is both painful and pleasurable. There are more crazy mothers than you might think. You can be having a professional lunch at a conference or with a colleague in another department, and one of you will mention, perhaps without even intending to, that she has a crazy mother. Oh, she will say to you or you will say to her, your mother was, uh, mentally ill? Yes, she was crazy, you will say. *Really* crazy? she will ask. (Many people will claim that their mothers are crazy when they do not know what they are talking about.) Yes, you will say, *really* crazy. Attempted suicide, anorexia, paranoia, violent, the whole bit. I had to commit her twice. A flash of recognition across the table, a sigh. So was mine. Yes, mine was too.

What follows is a conversation that no one else can possibly follow. It is made up of codes, silences, sighs, pauses. The first question: Is she dead (yet); code, are you still going through this? The second question: What about the rest of the family? Gone you say. My brother and I have not seen each other since the funeral. My sister calls when it snows at home; she is unaccountably excited by snow. Ah yes, my friend will say. Yes, I know (silence). What about you, she says, how are you; code, do you sometimes feel crazy too, are you scared like me of becoming your mother? I'm okay now, you say. I kind of lost it—went over the edge and couldn't stop crying—after I committed her the second time. Therapy, antianxiety drugs, antidepressants, anti-everything. None of it helped. It's only time that helps, don't you think? Now I'm okay. Yes, I'm okay now, I think. Oh yes, she says, me too, but I'm still on the Prozac. Hope to get off soon. Sometimes it seems impossible to think about it all. Sometimes it is too much to believe.

Sometimes, though, such conversations give me pause. They make me think my mother wasn't so bad. She was just always wishing for snow and usually it didn't come. And when it came, it didn't stick.

One friend was adopted. In my opinion, she had a perfectly good mother and father. Why trouble the waters? They were crusaders for civil rights during the fifties and sixties. They endured early morning phone calls, threats about crosses being burned on their property. They were parents to be proud of. I wished they were mine. When my friend got older, she wanted to find her birth mother. Her adopted parents, being the good people they were, gave her the information she needed, and she found her mother and her sister. Both were schizophrenic. Now I know why I've felt so crazy all my life, she says; it's kind of a relief.

A colleague tells me that when she was four her mother, who was an alcoholic, almost killed her two-year-old sister by starving her to death. My friend remembers the doctor storming into the apartment and yelling at her mother: "You've got to feed this baby or I'm going to take her away. You've got to *feed this baby!*"

Another friend believes that she was tortured by her father and some other people in secret ceremonies associated with their church in a small western town. When she was little, she would be awakened in the middle of the night and taken from her bed to a room with bright lights. Her mother, did she know? Now my friend is afraid of electrical wiring. She remembers something about fur and feathers.

ON THE DEATH OF A BLUEJAY

He was a jaunty fellow,
a bright and talky fellow.
He did me no harm.
A few berries here and there,
acorns snitched from squirrels
(who sometimes shared his fate)
and nuts stashed away in the eaves.
For the love of pecans
he was shot down in midflight
and lies festering beneath the tree.

I think of Icarus
gutstrung between earth and heaven
like a speck of red dust itching the eyeball
of the universe.

Gold-singer, dream-squawker
with a yen for nuts and bolts.
Tinkerer, tailor, candlestick-maker
with hot wax shrouding his wings.

Sun-streaker, moon-tamer
prancing on a pinhead,
breaching the walls of heaven.

ERIN CLAYTON PITNER

Dear Erin Dear Mama, I tell you if I had had to choose a crazy mother it would have been you.

palinode: 1. an ode or poem written to retract something said in a previous poem. 2. a retraction.

IX

Wednesday December 10, 1930

Every body is getting a little bit mystries now. Mother
asked which doll I liked best in a pile of dolls in Mongom-
trey Wards. And Jane Sturt and Mama had come back
from town saturday afternoon and I happened to be fooling
with some packages they had bought and Jane Sturt said:
you better not be fooling with those packages we have been
Christmas shopping and we might have something for you.
She said it so real I relly do believe she did.

Thursday December 11, 1930

Miss Olio kept me in so long that it knocked me out of
seeing the picture show. I think we are going to buy a
radio. It is a R.C.A. I think I will die if we don't get it.
I love it to death.

Saturday December 13, 1930

I didn't get to write anything yesterday. I wanted to tho.
I have been Christmas shopping. I didn't get to finish so I
am going again tonight with mother. I have gotten up all
of my lessons.

Monday Dec. 15, 1930

I forgot to write anything yesterday but that was not because I didn't want to. I have bought all but two of my Christmas presents. Those are Miss Olivos and mothers. Goodbye until tomorrow.

X

ASHES

Sorrow
is pain charred
to ashes still glowing
as old wounds crusting and bleeding
once more.

ERIN CLAYTON PITNER

After my mother had been undergoing chemotherapy for several months, her skin became irritated and sensitive. She began to cut up bits of soft material and put them wherever her clothes chafed her skin, around her waist, at the neck. She was down to seventy-five pounds, but she made me go out and buy her giant cotton underpants at Sears, which she secured with safety pins at the waist. As her skin got worse, she got crazier, or perhaps it was the other way around, I don't know. She began to cut more and more pieces of fabric smaller and smaller. She stuffed them everywhere, along with torn Kleenexes and cut-up handkerchiefs. She could not get things soft enough. When she would get up and walk, pieces of fabric, Kleenexes, and anything else she had thought to stuff into her clothes, would go flying. She would walk down the long hall with bits and pieces drifting lazily out of the bottom of her slacks and blouse. She would be losing pieces everywhere she went, and my daughter and I would walk along behind her picking them up and trying to give them back to her.

"Mama," I would say, "why do you stick all these pieces of material in your clothes when you know they are going to fall out?"

"It hurts," she would say. "You don't understand what it's like. The skin gets raw. Nothing helps. Nothing."

Several Octobers ago, as the cranes passed over, I became fainthearted at the prospect of inheriting Erin Taylor's ovaries. Frolicking like playful porpoises between my pelvic bones, my own duo insisted on playing hide and seek with the ultrasound technician. It occurred to me that these frisky ovaries might be out to get me. By the first of the year, I had enough of their antics, and so had everyone else who was trying to keep up with their whereabouts. After my surgery, my trussed belly was so tender that I stuck pieces of Kleenex into my pajama bottoms to keep the fabric from rubbing. I cut the elastic in my underwear.

One morning soon after I'd gotten home from the hospital, I was hobbling down the hall to the bathroom when I heard a sound behind me. It was my daughter, who had come to help out. "Oh, no," she was saying looking down at the floor aghast. "Oh *no*." I looked on the floor behind me and saw the bits and pieces of tissue. She picked them up and handed them to me. "Don't do that," she said and her voice sounded as if it had been caught on a nail. "Just don't do that."

"Oh, God," I said, genuinely horrified. Was I too coming to pieces? Then Carol began to laugh, and after a while I did too, holding my poor spliced belly for dear life.

I did not believe my mother when she said nothing would help. I thought there should be lotions ointments pills. There should be things to prevent this ultrasensitivity. All she had to do was call the doctor and get something. We did, and he sent her pills and ointments, but she was right. Nothing helped. It never did.

Pieces of something, fragments of a poem on the back of a Natchez Trace guide, fall from Erin's notebook. I pick them up, though there is no one to return them to.

> Last night
> I dreamt you, Mother.
> We roamed the house
> together, seeking something
> lost or stolen as dream-
> meanderers are prone to do.
> A coin, a button, a mirror, a scrap
> of paper, a hieroglyphic of
> the house. Spell bound,
> entranced, we map out
> each room like children pretending—
> blind man's bluff.
> Our fingers, recalling
> the dream, absorbing it
> with our flesh, with fingertips
> like shock waves groping
> chaotic bits and pieces
> flashing upon the retina of time
> like a mirror with the sheen half-crazed,

a frozen pond of glass where
time holds me icelocked
within its spell.
Etched about
with snowflakes
at Christmas
in candleglow.

I am a writer and literary critic. I know that these are the pieces but not the poem. I want Erin to come back and take these pieces (See how neatly I have typed them, Mother, correcting your spelling, selecting my favorites of your alternate words, making a line adjustment here and there). I want Erin to gather up all these pieces (Mother, after all, they are your responsibility, not mine), and make the poem.

Dear Erin Pitner:
I am writing to request some vital information from you, and I hope that you will respond as quickly as possible on this urgent matter. Please answer the following questions for me:

1. When did you reach the point that everything was in pieces?

2. What forces took you to that point? (Please list in order of importance.)

3. Do you know where the lost pieces can be located?

4. What preventative measures against further losses would you recommend?

Please do not feel that you have to limit yourself to these questions. Anything you can tell me will be most helpful.

Let me thank you in advance for a prompt and full

response to my queries. Please send me this information
at your earliest convenience.

> Sincerely,
> Minrose Gwin
> Professor

Dear Professor Gwin:

Who put me on your mailing list? My daughter the feminist?
Well, let me tell you, my life wasn't so bad. Pieces are like
snowflakes; they touch you in a way nothing else can, and
then they melt and are forever gone. I just wish I had had
more fun.

> Sincerely,
> Erin Clayton Pitner
> Poet

When my mother and the salesman had been married for
twenty-five years, my mother informed me that she wanted an
anniversary celebration and that it was my job to put one together.

"I just want to have a good time," she said gravely on the
phone. "I just want it to be fun."

Found in the move to Albuquerque: worn graduate semi-
nar notebook, fall 1976. Course title: William Faulkner's Novels. On one page about halfway through my notes: "In *Absalom, Absalom!* the father's silence signifies a lack of love and
humanity." Up and down the margins of the same page:

- Call caterer.
- Flowers? yes   centerpiece for table just a small one —
  maybe chrysanthemums
- Rex Plaza   private dining room

- Get silver bowl engraved "25th anniversary 11-4-76 from the children"
- 6 p.m.? $100.00 plus tax and tip. Can we charge? Yes(!)

No fun at the party, Mama. We sit around the table peering at one another around the tall mums (for the fall anniversary) in the centerpiece. My brother seems out of breath. My sister is late. She says her shift had to work overtime. My husband gives a toast to which everyone responds with blank looks; my daughter whines that she has a stomachache and cannot eat. I want to make a toast but you won't let me. Only men can make toasts, you say. You and I laugh too much. We eat steaks and drink the bottle of champagne, which is too soon gone; there should have been more, but my husband and I couldn't afford it.

The salesman is grimly silent. No one knows why. This is the bridegroom who wrote a letter to the perfect girl on their wedding day in 1951.

My Dearest

This is sort of a thank you note.

You may think I am not very excited about our wedding today and to an extent of being nervous and unsure, you would be right.

So many people talk about marriage as the start of a new life. I agree to that, but in addition, I am thinking today that it is the end, the culmination of the old one. Many wonderful things have happened to me in the old life, but the search, the quest for the perfect girl was long and hard.

However, there was never one instant of doubt in my mind that I would find her.

Today I am one of the happiest of men and so very much in love with you.

I just want you to know that when you stand there beside me this afternoon. I will wonder that this lovely and gentle lady is to be my wife and I will be enormously proud.

Now the groom, twenty-five years later, wears his sports jacket like a leper's skin. He picks up his fork, touches his food with it, and lays it down on the side of his plate. The less he says the louder you and I get. He looks so angry I am afraid he is going to snatch up the monster mums, which I've grown to loathe over the course of the evening, and throw them at us. The dinner is over by seven-thirty. My husband and daughter and I prepare to flee the scene of what has become a crime.

You look bewildered. "Come on over to the house for coffee," you plead. "We can visit."

"We're tired," we say. "Tomorrow we'll come." My husband and I collapse on the bed in the hotel room and drink bourbon and watch TV. Our daughter, who is seven, cries herself to sleep because we forgot the mums.

Fifteen Things the Salesman Never Did in My Presence:

1. Talk for more than five minutes about anything but politics and conservative causes.
2. Cook out in the backyard.
3. Throw or catch a ball.
4. Go swimming, fishing, or hiking.
5. Sing.
6. Dance.
7. Play a musical instrument.

8. Cook.
9. Wash clothes.
10. Dust or vacuum.
11. Tell a joke or laugh at one.
12. Have a beer.
13. Call to chat.
14. Throw a party.
15. Mow the grass.

Right after the salesman snatched my mother and me from the stronger-than-a-tornado house and set us down in the succession of places that could have blown away in an instant, he began to play a game with me. Usually it would happen when I was being loud or fussy. He would get a tight smile on his face, roll up a piece of newspaper and grab me by the arm. Then he would swat me all over like it was a joke, saying if I was going to cry he'd give me something to cry about since I was such a crybaby. I would jump around and try to laugh but would end up screaming bloody murder, and then my mother, who would be watching and laughing too, would say, oh, stop that now, you two. It is odd that I remember this happening on Sunday mornings with the sun coming through the windows and piles of newspaper on the floor; perhaps this is when they got a newspaper, or maybe it was simply when he was home.

I learned years later, from a bitter letter he wrote me at the end of his life, that she had told him never ever to hit me. And he never did, except in fun. What I remember is that he would stand over me and tremble all over with wanting to, even when I was in my thirties and forties, even in hospital corridors and in the waiting rooms of lawyers' offices. The letter he wrote was six pages typed single spaced. It came in response to my publishing Erin's book of poems. I stopped reading after the second page, in which he likened me to the first Minrose, my grandmother, whom he likened to a Vietcong torturer of U.S. soldiers in the past war.

What a strange comparison, I thought. How did he ever think it up? Whom did she torture with her sweet smile and her insistence on *amo, amas, amat*? (In a newspaper clipping on her students' latest sweep of the state Latin tournament, the young ones stand around her proprietarily, like ducklings. Their hands hover around her shoulders and arms; she has her hand on one boy's knee as if to say she is particularly proud of this special one. At a literary conference several years ago, a retired professor came up to me to tell me that he had taken my grandmother's Latin classes in high school. Not satisfied with two years of them, he and other members of the second-year class petitioned the school board for a third year, which, he said, was denied, but she taught the students anyway, in her spare time. When, in my own high school career, two friends and I were caught in a scheme to correct one another's answers while grading the others' papers in our second-year Latin class, my teacher, who lived three houses down the street from my then-retired grandmother, told me that, if she ever caught me doing such a thing again, she would tell "Miss Minrose," as she called her. The blood ran from my head at the thought. I could see the puzzled look that would come over my grandmother's face, the disbelief turning to sorrow that *amo, amas, amat* had been so desecrated, and by her own namesake, her first-born grandchild.) It is only now that I think about Eva and the apricot cakes, the social security, and the old hats, though this is not what the salesman meant.

The salesman did teach me to drive, not knowing of my earlier aborted lesson. He himself drove constantly; he was a good driver though riding with him was wearing on a person because he was always pushing on the accelerator in short jerks as if angry with it. Nor did he like to stop unless the gas tank were empty; on the road he seldom ate, though at each fill-up he would get a cup of coffee and pour sugar into it until it filled up half of the cup. Then he would gulp it down, no matter how hot it was.

The way he taught me to drive was this: he took me out on the highway, made me get up to sixty or so and then told me to run off the road onto the shoulder. We would do this for hours; finally I got so that I could do it without shaking all over. He would sit next to me with a half-smile on his face, as if he were having pleasant memories. Several times over the years I have silently thanked him for teaching me to pull to the shoulder at high speeds, especially when someone like my mother on her sixtieth birthday would come barreling across the line. Maybe he saved my life, I will think.

When I was in high school, he took me out on such a driving lesson and told me to turn down a gravel road leading into the woods. We bounced along for a while, in silence as usual. He had one of those centaur-looking vehicles that was a car in the front and a pick-up truck in the back, where he would load his pipe valves and fittings to take on the road to the oil refineries and such. When we got to the end of the road, he unlocked the glove compartment and pulled out a revolver. I didn't know there was a gun in the glove compartment, nor did I know what he intended to do with it. Then he told me to get out of the car; he wanted to teach me how to shoot a gun. I told him I didn't want to learn, but he told me it was for my own good.

Everybody needed to learn to shoot a gun. You never know when you might have to.

He handed me the gun and told me to point it into the woods. It was a hot day and the woods were green and buzzing with animal life. The pistol felt both hot and cold at the same time. I was afraid I was going to hit a squirrel or something or someone, but I was more afraid of him, so I listened to his directions (I couldn't say now what they were) and I squeezed the trigger and something happened in the trees, and that was that. Then we got back in the car and went home. He told me not to tell my mother about the gun, and I added that to my list of the many things I would not tell her.

When my sister was a girl, she loved to ride and wanted a pony. A friend of my mother who lived on the outskirts of town offered one as a gift, and my mother sent the salesman to pick it up in an old pickup he had at the time. On the way home the pony, not having been properly tethered, jumped out of the back of the pickup truck onto the highway. At that point, we found out later, my stepfather became furious and tied what was left of the injured pony to the back of his truck and pulled it, bucking and rearing, down the road.

My mother, my sister, and I were out in the front yard waiting for the pony. My sister was chewing her lip and dancing around. She had been up since dawn. We heard the truck with its crumbling muffler coming down the street and ran to the curb as if to watch an oncoming parade. The salesman was jamming the clutch, jerking the truck forward bit by bit, half-dragging, half-pulling the struggling pony, wild-eyed, bleeding, and foaming at the mouth. Neighbors were gawking and shaking their heads. "Poor thing," my mother, my sister, and I said in unison as he hit the brakes, causing the pony to slam its muzzle into the back bumper of the truck. "Poor thing, hell," he said. He jumped out of the truck and grabbed the rope. "Come on you," he said to the animal. He pulled it into the yard. "There's your damn pony," he said to my sister, rubbing his lips where his own spittle had crusted over. The pony stood there swaying, its breath coming in forced rattles. Its mouth was torn at the corners. Its eyes rolled back.

My sister stood there looking at the bloody pony. Her arms dangled at her sides like bent sticks. A straight lock of hair had fallen over her eyes. Then she reached out and touched it on the neck. It started violently. She looked ashamed. The pony recovered, but she rode it only a few times. Finally my mother found someone who lived in the country to take it, and the pony disappeared as if it had never been there.

The salesman also dragged me down the road, but it was for my own good, my mother said later. It was right after I had graduated from college. I wanted to get a job on a newspaper, but I had insisted on majoring in English instead of journalism because I could read more books. My professors in the latter department, understandably I suppose, did not feel compelled to try to place me as they had many of their majors. So I went home for the summer and worked in the department store I usually worked in. I had friends there, older ladies who had been in lingerie or shoes for twenty or thirty years. They didn't mind it, they said, and neither, I found, did I. We had our excitements. Once, during the lunch hour, a woman came in a side door, went to the wig counter, piled a dozen or so wigs on top of her head, placed both hands on top of the pile, and ran out the door with them just as I was wondering why she liked to wear wigs by the dozen. Mostly, though, I would read my novels, which I had placed strategically behind the scarf counter. I had sent out resumes by the dozens but had not gotten so much as a phone call.

One hot night late in July the salesman said to me, "I'm going to the Gulf Coast tomorrow. You come on with me, and let's see if you can't get a job down there." I could tell that this was not a request.

The next day we set out in his truck, which was empty in the back and therefore clattering. By early afternoon, he delivered me to the front of the looming *New Orleans Times-Picayune* building and dropped me off. "I'm picking up some valves. I'll be back in a couple of hours," he said. "Go on in there and talk to them."

A receptionist behind a glass window was as far as I got ("You don't have an appointment?" she asked, raising a carved eyebrow). I shoved a rolled-up resume through the slot under the glass and fled. I spent the next hour and forty-five minutes standing in front of the building waiting to be picked up. People coming and going were starting to look at me oddly when my stepfather finally drove up.

I leapt into the truck, now piled high with enormous pipe valves. I was trying not to cry. "If I'd had time to call first," I said.

He didn't answer but pulled over at the first phone booth. "They've got a big newspaper over there in Mobile," he said. "Call them and tell them you'll be there in the morning. Set something up."

I got out of the truck like an animal going to slaughter. I got information on the line and asked for the *Mobile Press Register.* When I got the paper, I asked for the managing editor, and to my complete astonishment, a gruff voice came on the line and said, "This is Maurice." I poked a finger in my spare ear to hear above the traffic and told Maurice I was passing through Mobile and needed a job. I was a college graduate and I had clips. Maurice said to come on by.

That afternoon the salesman took me to Maison Blanche department store and bought me a red dress. Then he checked us both into the Monteleone Hotel in the French Quarter. The only rooms left were the King's Room and Queen's Room, so we stayed in them. The Queen's Room was a dark blood red and gold. That night he took me to an oyster bar and showed me how to eat raw oysters on saltine crackers with a mix of ketchup, horseradish, and lemon on top. "Some people don't like to swallow them whole," he said, "so you put them on top of crackers to give you something to bite into."

By the time I got to Maurice's door the next morning, I had walked through a newsroom full of men clacking away at their typewriters. Most had cigarettes smoldering in ashtrays on top of their desks. They looked so flocklike, all of them perching about, that they reminded me of Uncle Vann and his cronies clustered like pigeons on the courthouse stoop under the wings of the Temperance Lady. There was indeed one older sober-faced woman working off to the side, on the society section I learned later. I walked into Maurice's office — I had on my new dress — and told him I could do the work just as well as any of those guys out there. Better. It was 1967 and I knew I had to be emphatic; I had to say it up front and get it out of the way. I threw my clips from the student newspaper and my resume on his desk. Maurice looked astonished by me. The interview ended quickly. I was sure I had failed some unspecified test, but by the time we bumped into the driveway at home, I lightheaded with exhaust fumes and relief, my mother appeared smiling at the door. Maurice had called.

Now it is 1981 and my mother is telling me she is afraid. She does not tell me her aging husband is locking himself in the back room to roar like a lion and make choking noises like the Chipmunks on the radio or exotic birds jabbering in nonhuman time. She is not specific. She tells me she thinks he is crazy and he scares her. She is spinning through her sixtieth summer, and she is getting tired of nobody talking to her. She is tired of the flatness in the bread. She tells me she is ready to take to the road. She just wishes the car would stop running off in strange directions and getting itself all bent up. She is poised for flight, but every route she can think of circles back.

A NOTE TO WALLACE STEVENS

I don't want to count blackbirds.
They make me think of crows
and crows eat corn

and filch the eyes
from leftover scarerogues
which bring to mind vultures

to finish off the carcass
of the hound clumped
beside the field.

I like to think of cardinals and bluebirds.
The kind that leave cheery clawprints
on pink and lavender cards

sent to hospices to urge along
ninety year olds and remind them
of home.

And I recall tiny blue butterflies
gleaning the last dregs
of August

before they leave for Argentina
to become fodder for the blackbirds and crows
plundering the late sweet corn.

ERIN CLAYTON PITNER

It is 1982 and Erin, having survived the wreck of her sixtieth birthday and now gainfully employed raising and lowering the Park Service flag at the Natchez Trace Visitors' Center, is still swerving back and forth over the line between coming and going. She is looking for a small apartment. She whispers into the phone that she wants a legal separation. He is hitting her, she says, but no one must know. I don't know what to think. I write her useless letters, cards with hippos turning cartwheels to cheer her up.

When things get crummy,
I still want my mummy.

Dear Mama,
Hope things aren't getting you down too much.
Love, Minrose

She writes back that she needs to get away. She comes to visit me carrying her three-inch-thick dictionary like a shield.

"You didn't have to cart that thing all the way. *I* have a dictionary," I say when she climbs off the bus, her Webster's held over her heart, "several dictionaries."

"I *write* in it," she says, clutching it as if I am going to snatch it and run. "I mark the words I want, and when I use them in a poem, I put a star by them."

"Oh," I say, not knowing what else to say. I am having my own problems with words. I have quit smoking and am trying to write my dissertation. This is not a good time for a visit. I have become an incessant worrier, and now I am worried about my mother needing a place to live. I stay up late pounding my dissertation about women who hate and envy one another, the white enslaving the black, onto a manual typewriter, throwing the carriage so hard that my tax-roll shoulder has resumed its aching. I am thinking about the first Minrose and Eva, now both lying in the same cemetery but far from each other, separate but unequally dead, since one had thirty more years than the other and didn't have to worry about making up the blood. I am seeing the sway of wagons coming from South Carolina, and those who walked beside them. And there is Miss Erin's peculiar whiteness to ponder.

My mother never told me about Lathree Barlow. Lathree unfolded unexpectedly in the bits and pieces of dusty paper on my card table. First I found the explanation for a poem dedicated to her which my mother presumably read on some occasion. Then I discovered the published poem itself, "Crossing the Line," originally entitled "Black on White." There is also one extant letter from Lathree to my mother, dated August 17, 1964. There is Erin Taylor's diary when she was nine years old, wishing for snow and Lathree. These are the pieces of evidence that make the story.

Insofar as I can discern, the facts of the story are as follows: A young black woman named Lathree took care of Erin Taylor when she was little, in the 1920s. Then Lathree and a young man named Toby, lover or husband I do not know, like the mythic flying Africans of slavery times who took off from the cotton and rice fields, sped away with all due haste, leaving mean Jim Crow eating their dust. Lathree and Toby went either to Detroit or Chicago, but eventually ended up in Chicago. (I hesitate on this point because my mother may not be telling the truth, or may be mistaken in her poem when she says Lathree went to Detroit; the 1964 letter from Lathree comes from Chicago. I do not trust my mother on any of the facts in question.) Little Erin Taylor loved Lathree and, having lost her, missed her terribly. Little Erin Taylor was convinced that Lathree missed her terribly too. The adult Erin Taylor was convinced that Lathree was unhappy Up North. Lathree wrote to Erin Taylor over the years, well into my mother's adulthood, and the two saw each other over the years when Lathree would come home to visit her family.

There are several lies, or errors, embedded in my pieces of evidence. The first is fairly obvious. Erin's poem about Lathree, written by my mother in her fifties, is dedicated to a "Laurie Lee," as are Erin's handwritten notations that introduce the poem. This is not exactly a lie. It is a mistake. Erin the poet has forgotten Lathree Barlow's name; one does not dedicate a poem to someone and change her name in the process. I can think of no explanation except forgetfulness. (It is to be hoped that Erin's mental lapses were even then manifesting themselves.) The other lies, or mistakes, you can discover for yourself. The texts in question are as follows:

1. The Introduction/Explanation of the Poem (in Erin's handwriting):

> Black on White
> For Laurie Lee
> A poem about one child's relationship to someone she loved dearly and about how their inevitable separation affected her—*in retrospect.* What I actually remember is walking up a dusty road with her on the last night before she left, crying— This was my very first separation from someone I loved so very much. ["so very much" crossed out] But it is also about the unique relationship between black & white in the South when I was growing up. Only a Southerner can really understand a relationship such as this.

2. The Published Poem:

> CROSSING THE LINE
>
> *for Laurie Lee*
>
> We sat at table together
> sharing the same earthenware bowl
> of collard greens and cornpone
> long before time caught up to us
> in pages of bloody script.
>
> You were young and lissome,
> darkly gold as a Tahitian,
> breath sweet as hibiscus
> as you sang me to sleep
> dreaming of drowsy blue waters

and an outrigger of our own
drifting beyond the stars—
I clutched your hand.

When I was nine
you left with *him* on the dawnbound bus
for Detroit, swearing to return
and you did every summer
only to leave again, torn
between the two of us.
You and Toby making it alone
in the smog and gloom of the city
without a thimbleful of earth
to call home.

You lived in a coldwater flat
five floors up—your lovely skin ashen,
your face a dark grimace of despair.

"They treat us like dogs,"
you said.

                ERIN CLAYTON PITNER

3. Letter from Lathree Barlow to Erin Taylor Clayton Pitner:

                                    Chicago, Ill.
                                    Aug. 17 1964

Dear Mrs Erin Taylor
Just a few line to let you hear from me after such a long
delay but with me not so well in and out of the Hospital i
didn't want to get some body else to ans your sweet letter so
nice of you to make me such a offer Mama not so well but i

will appreciat any thing you will do for me or Mama it not
necessary for her to come back for i have Lunit and Annie
Mae both with me and she getting feeble and she dont like
up her time she stay a week or so she wonder how Ben and
his family and the rest getting along so i want her to be
happy how is your sweet little family fine i do hope please
look over me for waiting so long to write but i love you as i
alway did how is your sweet mother getting fine i hope i can
picture you being little girl with snow ball the cat he Scratch
us if he see a dog you had a little doll house and we would
have more fun (Smile) Give my love to Miss Linda and her
family also Mr Stewat and his family I will alway remain the
same toward you all with all my love

Lathree

Two decades later, writing my dissertation and thinking
about Lathree and Eva and two Minroses and two Erins (does
it take two of us to equal one of them?), I am acquiring, in the
absence of my Winstons, a taste for Jim Beam on the rocks. I
am thinking I can imagine Lathree and Toby, maybe right before dawn, on a Sunday morning—let's say it's 1930, let's say
it's summer and the pavement below has just begun to cool
down from the sizzle. They're slowly climbing the five flights of
steps, leaning on each other and giggling to themselves and
humming a tune from the Duke. Maybe they're thinking that
cold water is sure going to feel good on the skin. They are worn
out after a night of lindy-hopping and a few nips from the bottle in the juke joint down the street. Plus they're hungry, and
maybe Lathree is thinking about the eggs and grits and that
leftover redeye gravy she was saving for supper. Maybe she's
thinking to hell with supper.

I sit at my kitchen table at two in the morning watching the ice melt into muddy pools in my glass. My mother, my family, has become a research problem I am trying to solve, but the problem and the conclusion, the lie and the truth, are the same thing.

In Erin's college notebook with the football player on the cover (carrying the ball, assumably to a touchdown because he looks so pleased with himself) and my father's name scrawled all over the margins is the following outline in my mother's careful script:

RESEARCH PAPER:
  I. Statement of the Problem
    1. What *(I roll the ice cubes around the edge of my glass and write: My mother is going crazy.)*
    2. Why *(Marriage to the salesman? Physical abuse? Social pressure? Genes? Because she wants to? Because the words don't fit the thing? Because Lathree left? Because she can't remember Lathree's name?)*
    3. Where *(At home and abroad.)*
    4. When *(Whenever she feels like it.)*
  II. Methods of Analysis *(Direct observation by self and others.)*
  III. Presentation of Data *(Stealing flowers off church altar. Driving on wrong side of road. Acquired taste for prescription medicines. Strange attachment to dictionaries.)*
  IV. Summary & Conclusions *(My mother is going crazy. Maybe I am too.)*

The Erin of the early eighties has company. Her men friends are in despair. These are men my mother has met prowling the county library or in writers' "round robins." Or men she has

never met but who read her poems and wrote her first. Fan letters, she called them.

From the friend waiting for the perfect poem:

Dear Erin,
I'm sorry I haven't written sooner but I've been having a
two month bout with depression; there seems to be no end
in sight, so I decided to write anyway. It's hard to admit failure, and I've failed grandly. Where do I go from here? . . .

From an older man, recently diagnosed with Alzheimer's,
whose wife will write my mother six months later to say that
his mind is all but gone. Soon, if they are lucky, he will be in
the veterans' hospital.

Dear Erin:
Thank you for your letter of Sept. 4. I'm sorry to be so
long in replying—but I'm still not in normal (for me) to-
getherness. An awkward expression—but I'm sure you
know what I mean. I haven't yet returned completely to
myself—whoever that is. But this is a sign of improvement
—no that's not all: I don't expect to recover "myself" again
—but at least a livable version may be possible. . . . Sorry,
but simply can't write a voluble letter as used to do. But it
will be worth the value of "Hello—hope life is serving you
better." I'm working on a poem (short); and when it's
finished, as I will be, I'll send you a copy.

Then, for Erin, the mutation. The strangeness of the one becomes the strangeness of the many. A friend speaking of ovarian cancer says it is like a climber throwing the rope. Rope
after rope goes out to anchor the far places, the intestines point

by point, the liver, the lungs. All those little ropes being thrown out helter-skelter, catching what they can catch.

Like the black widow spider, it makes an ugly messy web. But very strong.

When my mother found out she had cancer, she returned to the salesman and plunged headlong into a place the words couldn't reach. She never wrote again, or so she said. I may have evidence to the contrary. Inside a large envelope with the scrawled words "*FUNERAL* E T Pitner" centered on the front, Erin has left directions for her funeral. Without preamble, on sheets of white stationery:

My funeral should be like this—in church—a worship service but choir in place—no marching in and out. Choir singing because music means so much to me. Hymns: Beneath the Cross of Jesus, Zion Stands with Hills Surrounded, This is my Father's World [crossed out], Fairest Lord Jesus & organist to play My God and I Walk through the Fields Together.

Bible passages—
Ps. 19. 1–6
Ps. 50. 1–6
Ps. 27 & Ps 25. 1–8
Hebrews Chapt. 11. 1–3
Romans. Chapt. 9. 31–39
John—Chapt. 1. 1 thru 5
John—Chapt. 14. 1 thru 7, 27 & 28
I Cor. 15. 20–26, 54–58
I Tim. 1:17
Rev. 21: 3, 4

John — I know that my redeemer liveth and that He shall
    stand upon the latter day of earth.
Micah: What does the Lord require of thee but to do justly,
    to love mercy & to walk humbly with thy God. [all this
    marked out]
From Thomas Wolfe read:
    Someday I shall die; I know not where — I go to find a
    place more large than home

Following these directions and, to my taste, rather odd
Bible readings for her peaceful passage, which would have
made Erin's funeral among the longest in Protestant history, is
a draft of a poem, scrawled on the same paper in the same pen.
It is not a poem to be read aloud at one's funeral. Even its line
breaks make it seem violently torn from some other unspeak-
able thing.

No place to hide
from the leer of the sun
searching out every pothole,
every dream denied.
That virulent green of the
meadow is already beginning
to fade
the roses shrink from
the promise of beauty denied them by
the cool mist of rain
on a wedding day
where the sun glares
down like the worried frown
on the bridegroom's face.
Will the sun never go down

on their love? Will the
white lace dress never assemble
& fade like the Cape Jasmine in
her bridal bouquet?
Already the kids are restive,
on their knees in the
dust like jackanapes with
begrimed faces sweating
oivulets of clay. Melting
away in the blue distance
with the sun battering
them to pillars of clay.

I don't know when Erin wrote her funeral directions and her poem about worried bridegrooms (the salesman by his own admission?), melting children (whose but hers?), and pillars of clay (what we all became in the end). Perhaps it was after the cancer, when she was determined not to die but knew that she probably would, or perhaps before, when she was determined not to live but still alive enough to run off the road or ponder the long brown arm of the river called Old Man.

It was when my hair started falling out. I was reading the Encyclopedia then. That was all I could read. I was reading about the boy Dionysus Zagreus, the son of Zeus and Persephone. How the Titans dismembered the boy and ate him up, all but the heart, which Athena saved and gave back to Zeus who for reasons I don't understand swallowed it whole. I felt swallowed whole, like that warm heart. So I wrote up my own funeral. Then I felt better.

❄ ❄ ❄

After I had committed my mother to Whitfield, I located the salesman, who had left town and then resurfaced after the proceedings were over and after my mother had been removed from her home and sent on her unwilling journey. I asked him about her allegations. Why was she saying these things about him, that he hit her? "Yeah I have to knock her around a little every now and then just to get her attention," he said, rubbing his mouth. When he said this, I noticed for the first time how one could see straight through his blue eyes into a space where there was nothing but a startling vacancy. I wondered what was beyond that space—was it a father placing himself carefully on the doctor's examining table, fingering the pistol under his coat? Those towheaded brothers with their eggshell skulls?

I did find a local lawyer after several tries (nobody wanted the case, whether from fear or distaste I do not know). I tried to get custody, guardianship it was called, of my mother (though she and her craziness were the last things I wanted to be responsible for) and was told by the lawyer (a team of them, actually, who sat around a long shiny table with me) that this would be almost impossible if (a) she did not want me to have it (she was too far gone by then to have an opinion) or (b) he did not want me to have it (which he did not). The best my lawyer could do was to write a letter of warning to the salesman. This was accomplished, at a cost of almost a thousand dollars.

The letter of warning must have dispatched my lover the shelf, who came flying out of the wall toward me as sweetly and urgently as if returning home from a long trip. I could touch my neck brace and say, "Enough, I quit." Tuck myself into bed for many months, fully documented, I will hasten to point out, by doctors' orders, workers' compensation, medical leave, physical therapy records. (I have the papers, Erin, to prove it.)

How convenient, when you were the only one who knew what it was that was happening, when you were the only one who could have cut the rope and pulled me back.

Erin, you were tied too tight.

Blame me. That's a joke. There you were and everyone was saying what a shame that sweet baby girl has no father. I felt like something thrown away in that hot house. Ugly red brick square of a house that nothing, not even a tornado, could move. Tossing and turning at night. Daddy walking the halls making the floor creak. Everything always the same. I thought it would be all right, and sometimes it was at first when I was hungry for him after he'd been gone all week and he'd come in with that half smile on his face, like he had a surprise for me. He would look like that picture of him standing by his airplane ready for the runway with nothing but dark water beyond, ready for anything those Japs could dish out. I would have flown away with him anywhere he wanted to go. My stomach would turn over when he smiled like that.

THE AWAKENING

Your body white as a child's
warmer than my own
eyes still fragile with sleep
lips curved to mine
breathing you back
from your lost lane's end
of darkness

distant as death
beyond my dreaming.

Your morning breaks softly
into the sunlight
of my arms.

ERIN CLAYTON PITNER

It was what came after. All that work and never a word. After a while he stopped even the smiling. I thought it was my fault. I wanted to have picnics and be like everyone else. I just wanted to have some fun every now and then, like going out dancing and eating catfish or just to the picture show. I wanted him to read my poems and say Good, Erin Taylor, these are very good. Then everything I did seemed like too much and I felt like I was always flooding some dry place. Sometimes I could feel my insides cramping and flooding like a bad period. I thought I was going to fill up like a bucket and drown in my own blood. You could have gotten up off that bed and taken me in.

Some stories, having been told, are satisfied. Perhaps they produce a slight indentation on the brain, of which they become unaccountably proud, not realizing that such imprints are short-lived in the human species.

I have no such story for the last nine months of Erin's life, which, as any expectant mother knows, is a long time. I know that when her broken hip began to heal, Whitfield discharged her. I know that before she was discharged in 1988, she was given dozens of electroshock treatments that made her scrawlings on the backs of the torn envelopes, which materialized like dirty leftover bits of snow in my mailbox, look as if she were in the process of being electrocuted as she wrote them ("I want you to come and get me because I'm so tired what happened to you"). I know that I spoke with her psychiatrist several times by phone and once in person, and he said she was "making progress" and that the electroshock was helping. I know that after she left Whitfield, the salesman put her in Roselawn Retirement House, 118 South Glenfield Road, New Albany, Mississippi, where she was, by all accounts, a compliant patient. ("She died in peace," Jane Stuart of the Milk of Magnesia pronounced in a letter of condolence to the salesman. This was the same southern belle Jane Stuart who previously had written the skeletal Erin Taylor advising her to eat graham crackers to gain weight and go back to church "to make you feel more like yourself.") I know that sometime in that year, either before or after Erin's discharge from Whitfield, the cancer came out of hiding and her abdomen began to swell and had to be drained again and again. I know, though I would like to believe otherwise, that she did not open the cards and letters I sent to explain myself, my own injury. I was told and I believe that she died in transit, in the back of an ambulance. I know that the salesman had her funeral so soon thereafter that I almost wasn't able to get a flight in to go to it. I know that the coffin with the cornflowers was closed. I know that a neighbor woman, a busy someone I knew only slightly, asked me if I wanted to open the coffin to see my mother's face since it had been such a long time, and I became unaccountably afraid and said no, absolutely not.

Dear Santa Clause:
I love you so much, and Christmas too. Please bring me a little doll house with furniture, a tricycle, a jumping jack, and a white rabbit.

I will thank you so much if you will bring me these things.

Lots of love,
Erin Taylor Clayton

It is 1928, cold January, the first day of school in a new year. You are in the first grade. You got a white kitten for Christmas (perhaps a more obtainable surrogate for the white rabbit). You name him Snowball because in Mississippi you are always wishing for snow. He is still very small (though large enough to have made an impression on Lathree). The most beautiful cat, you tell me as I sit on your lap twenty years later. The most beautiful. Now he follows you to school like Mary's lamb. You look around and see him on the sidewalk behind you. You tell him to go home, and run the rest of the way to school. You look back to see him sitting there watching you go. You never see him again. He melts into the world and leaves you behind. More than a half century later you write of how he floated away

> into the leafless trees, the icy stubbled
> grass as if he had never been.
> A small white cat clawing his way back
> when the clematis begins to bloom.
> His eyes blazing green as the heartshaped
> leaves despite the withered canes
> of August

You died thinking I was your enemy. The August before your death in October, I press clematis in a book to dry them and send them to you.

※　※　※

Now it is 1991, another summer's end. In Mississippi the clematis are again blooming. This is the first of several summers to come in which I will try to write my mother's story. There is a day here at the end of this summer in New Mexico when I walk down by the Rio Grande and see pink thistle and Russian olive. As I walk, I know that back home in Mississippi the squirrels are gathering the acorns from the huge oak next to my mother's window, the one she would not let anyone cut though it cracked the walls, and putting them in neat piles along the side of the house. The air hums with gnats and mosquitoes. In Mississippi it is almost dark. The lightning bugs will soon be out.

Here in New Mexico the prairie dogs pop in and out of their holes beside the road. They stand on their haunches and look around. It is a deeply pleasurable look, the look they were born for, though they are skeptical about what it is possible to see and whether that which they fail to see will cause them harm.

Here it is late afternoon and dry, though we have had evening thunderstorms almost every day for two weeks. The limbs of our apple tree bend to the ground with fruit. Through some quirk of nature or human intervention, we're not sure which, the apple tree grows sideways, its trunk propped off the ground by its branches. From that warped position, it produces small misshapen green apples that are the best cooking apples I have ever tasted. This is because they are sour, but the sourness is not in the apple, which is naturally sweet, but in the apple's situation, the apple's fate to be on a broken tree that wants to live, that continues to grow and bloom and bear fruit. Concord grapes are falling silently from the vine; wasps buzz and drink.

Even here in the desert there is a heaviness to the air. My dog, who, though I do not know it yet, will die the following spring from eating nectarine pits, his belly swollen to twice its size, tosses an apple into the air from his mouth. It is caught by the cat, who flips and catches it on her claw, in one motion.

I try to place Erin in this scene. It is like trying to place the one essential piece in a puzzle, the piece that makes the picture move into shape so that you can see it for the first time. I cannot make the piece fit. My life takes its shape because of my mother's absence from it. But that shape is not anything I can see. It is instead a gesture, the way my dog cocked his head when I said his name a moment ago or now the birds settle in at the feeder, scratching and snuffling. It is the "whoosh" they make when the hawk circles. We have chamisa blooming here, but no clematis. I have cut back the iris from Minrose's yard. Perhaps they will do better next year, though the bind weed here is fierce and strong.

In Mississippi nothing is stirring. Maybe in your house, Erin, an old deaf man sits on the screen porch staring off into the distance smoking a cigarette. In a few years he will go to his high school reunion in a neighboring town and find there his high school sweetheart. They will marry and live happily ever after until his death a few precious years later. The house will cast off its evil spell and come alive. (Were you the evil one, Mother? Was I?)

The happy aged couple will have parties; they will be gay. Everyone will say, loudly, for his benefit, how nice, how *sweet.* Some will think, if only. Perhaps they will even play music, perhaps even your old Cole Porter records, Mother, just to make you toss restlessly in the cemetery down the street, like we used to toss and turn in our hot beds when the holy rollers would moan and cry out all night long, or when Pop Pop would walk.

But now, maybe later tonight, the old deaf man will leave on a trip, and no one will enter the house for days. A cobweb will form here, a dust ball there. Pictures of a lost family will hang on the walls of this silent house. Nothing will move except the shadows.

Maybe on the table by your chair still sits a dusty picture of you and me. We have on matching sundresses. You are in your late twenties and beautiful. You have dark hair to your shoulders and a full mouth. You lift your face to the camera and smile, but your eyes are looking somewhere beyond the lens. I sit in your lap. My hair is curly and blond, and my face is round and covered in freckles. I am about four years old. I squint at the sun. Our fingers are entwined. Your arm encircles my waist. The picture is in black and white and it shows our shadows on the ground.

Outside the house your clematis vine glides like an uneasy lover over and around and through the green trellis. A bee lights on one of the flowers and lifts off lightly into the dusk. (At this very moment, perhaps, a yellow jacket sucks blissfully on an open grape in my backyard; it is still daylight here, after all, well before dusk, when the yellow jacket will slip into its indiscernible slit in the hard dirt to take its rest.) On your street the crickets are starting to chirp. Moths float up from the trees. Lightning bugs flare one by one in the gathering dark.

Three blocks away, next to the cemetery, there is a softball game going on. Little boys struggle to hit the ball out into the cemetery and make their home run. They have learned that this is the way to win and they know the value of winning. They are silent. Several spit on their hands and rub them in the dust. Do the little girls still sit with their mothers and fathers and watch their brothers play this game? Do their light voices rise and fall in the growing dark? Does anyone hear what they are saying?

The moon is rising. In the cemetery next to the playing field, you lie under a flat headstone that can be mowed over by the big tractor mower they use. You lie inside the country woman's coffin with the blue cornflowers. The cornflowers are beginning to fade and you are waiting for the dawn so that you can drift away.

MISSISSIPPI MOON

The moon is hanging with the heavy hotness
of summer,
peering through the dusky windows
of the day,
burning the late embers
of August.
Like the flowing whiteness
of the summer sun
as it melts away the moisture
that runs
before the savage heat
of noon,
the moon is climbing,
shattering
the humid air
into incandescent showers of lightness,

blazing
across the terraced lawn
and the silent street,
stirring
the slow wind of midnight, and
running
before the dawn.

ERIN CLAYTON PITNER

Here in New Mexico I look out my window at the stippled
limbs of the giant sycamore. The hummingbird nest is now
empty. You cannot see it unless you know that it is there, on
its outward fork of limbs. Even if you know its location, have
looked at it countless times over many late summers, it takes a
sharp eye and serious attention to detail (there are many forks,
there are nodules that appear to be nests) to make it out. Such
precision is costly. You might miss, for example, the Sandia
Mountains turning hot pink, a sexy hot pink, in the last of this
day's sun. For a scruffy nest the size of an egg, you might miss
a spectacle of watermelon proportions.

Earlier today: I am standing by the elevators in a huge medical complex. A woman in a wheelchair looks like my mother.
She weighs maybe seventy pounds. She is leaning over the side
of the chair and moaning. "Take deep breaths," the orderly ad-
vises, and turns to talk to a nurse, who, I notice, has very white
teeth. The sick woman is wearing a wig of black hair, which is
topsy-turvy. I worry that if she leans over further it will fall off
and I will be in the embarrassing predicament of having to pick
it up and hand it back to her, or perhaps even help her situate

it on her head. Right now she couldn't care less about her wig. She is gray with pain and nausea. Her arms are ropes. I wait to take another elevator, but we end up on the same floor. Now she is crying in ragged breaths and being rolled into oncology. Her son, or someone who acts like a son, is waiting. The orderly deposits his charge deftly and flees, as if delivering a pizza. I am called for my appointment with a neurologist who I hope will cure the sudden onset of migraines I've been having.

When I return to the waiting room thirty minutes later, the woman in the wheelchair is still there. Suddenly she starts to wail and gag. Her son jumps up and begins to pound on the receptionist's desk. "For God's sake, she can't wait forever to see the doctor," he says in a clipped hurt voice, as if his vocal chords have been foreshortened. "She is too sick. Let me take her back to psychiatry so she can go to bed."

And I want to say: Here. Let me take her. Let me take her home and put her to bed and stroke her forehead and make her hot tea. I want to say: Let her be my mother for a while so that you and she can take a rest and I can lay down my own mother, whose head I did not hold.

Am I telling the truth? No. I do not say any of these things. I do not want this suffering dying mother in our house. I am grateful she is somebody else's.

In Mississippi, time has stopped. In New Mexico, time is still passing. Now it is late afternoon in late January a decade later. A millennium later. The sun cuts dapples of light across the sober fields at Bosque del Apache. Ten times the cranes have come and gone since I began this book. They are the oldest living bird species, sixty million years old. Ten years is nothing to them.

Soon it will be spring, again another nest of two eggs, again another crop of strange apples. Soon the cranes will murmur to one another. Pass the word, they will say without saying a word, it is almost time to leave this place. Watch for a sign. It is almost time to begin it.

SONG FOR BEGINNING

Christmas greens wilting   limp
as the year shriving itself
licking old wounds and griefs
gimping into oblivion.

Time is winnowed down
and reappears   angel-pure
crisp
as the slash of frosted wings
tingling in the wind   terse and clear.

Dull spirit hones itself
and sings
        life
soaring
to meet the cold flame of sun
poised
on the edge of morning.

ERIN CLAYTON PITNER

Some stories, having been told, float away like cottonwood fuzz. Sometimes they will drift down to a muddy place. But no one knows how or where until much later.

Go back now. 10:44 at night, though for all I care it could be morning. You don't want to be born. You want to stay. I keep trying to push you over the line. If I could cut my belly open right now and pull you from me, I would gladly do it, even if it killed you and me both. At long last it becomes easy, like a seizure, and you slip out like a stick of melty butter hardening when you hit the air, which you will catch and hold and scream back at me. Later they will bring you to me and you will take one look and start to cry like your heart is already broken. I will be afraid that you are going to be too much for me.

Above me the splitting and falling, then, all at once, the flight. Taste of blood and swampy flesh. Remember me.

You were too fair for the hot sun that first spring after you were born when everyone was so happy that the war was really over. I thought my sweet Al was on his way home and everything was going to be all right. I carried you around under an umbrella but still you would get red as a beet you were so fair. I did everything I could. I made you wear bonnets. I put a tent over your stroller when I took you out. And all the while we were just killing time, waiting for something to happen and your daddy to come on home so we could go to a colder place.

When my daughter was a few weeks old, one morning I fell asleep while nursing her in the bed. I awoke a few hours later to find her face next to mine on the pillow. She was gazing intently at me nose to nose as if imprinting on her memory the features of my face. In that moment I saw her knowledge of me in her eyes. I saw her flesh yearn for itself in me.

My daughter has a mole on the crown of her head. You cannot see it unless you part the hair and look carefully. Today I think about my daughter a thousand miles away in Virginia, and I know that she has that mole. I know how it grew fast one summer and I was afraid. I know that it bleeds when someone brushes her hair too hard because I have done it. I know that there is another mole on the left side of her neck. I remember how her fingers curled and uncurled around my finger when she drank from my breasts and how watchful her eyes were.

The October my mother died and I lay in bed looking out over the Blue Ridge and turning my electrodes on and off at twenty-minute intervals, I did not think I was going to recover. After we got back from my mother's funeral, my husband went down to the pound and brought me a black kitten. She was the smallest and quietest of the litter of a mother cat who had been run over. She was only three weeks old, and with her hair standing on end like dandelion fluff from worminess, she seemed perpetually shocked by life. She was very sick when I got her, and I fed her a special diet for weeks. Later I cooked chicken and rice for her every day because that was all her stomach could handle. She vomited often and farted constantly. In an effort at humor, I named her Blossom. She slept with me, and I carried her around the house in the pocket of my robe. She sat on my lap while I made her food and ate my own and while I sat on the toilet, the only reasons I got out of bed. She grew into a thin-coated, thin-bodied cat with a small head and bare patches between the eyes and ears. She has always looked old. As she enters old age, she is beginning to throw up again, in odd spots with much frightening ado, gagging and choking. She sits on my lap as I write this. Her paw is on my breast. I am hers. She has no doubt about this. Nor do I.

FOR A FRIEND DYING

Don't speak death. Not yet.
I bring you bread, your favorite,

rich with raisins
and regret for years displaced
between us.
You feign hunger
and choke down a morsel, a crumb.
I turn away, strangling on grief and love.

We grew together like weeds,
thick as woodland blossoms—
wild narcissus and pale pink trillium
in April,
sumac flickering among the hedgerows
of fall.
Brambles too, clawing our feet
and swamp root dense as the rampant cells
burgeoning in your lungs.

Remember the store on the corner?
Old Mrs. Warden clenching her teeth
on our nickels and dimes,
clinking them on the counter like dice.
She disclaimed us—eight year olds—
when trust was common coin.

Jawbreakers were two for a penny,
licorice whips five for a dime.
We drank lemon soda in clear green glass bottles
dripping from the cold box,
and strawberry pop frothing on your lips
like blood.

You cough and clutch my hand,
your eyes darkening to pain.

No one else knows where we found the May apples
nor how wild and sweet they grew.

Don't speak death. Not you.

ERIN CLAYTON PITNER

Some stories are never satisfied. They fly away only to return,
predictably, in their own good time, hungry to be told again.
Finding you on closet floors licking the crust from the lids of
jars, I thought my skin might break open like figs in summer. I
thought I might get you to take and eat and remember. But it
would not, and I could not.

*You were so fair I could never keep you from getting sunburned and
freckles everywhere. I had never seen such freckles on a baby. I used to
wonder how you would look if they all grew together. I put bonnets on
you but you always pulled them off you hated those bonnets on your
head hated anything that was tight. The Easter you got the stuffed rabbit big as you were bigger even I had the worst time getting you to pose
with the rabbit. Finally Eva said look it wasn't the rabbit you hated it
was the bonnet. I'd tied it too tight. No no no you kept on saying and
shaking your head but at first I didn't understand why. And that hair
where did you get that hair strawberry blond they called you. Then it
just got darker and straighter and finally the brightness was gone except
for it being wavy in the rain. I watched it happen and it made me sad
because I wanted you to keep that hair always though it was a mess to
keep nice. I'd get aggravated with you about it. I'd shampoo it and you'd
cry I'd brush it and you'd cry. What a crybaby I'd say to have such
pretty hair God should have given it to someone else and you'd say
Mama I wish he had. You cried too loud that was the problem all that*

noise and no harmony and Al never coming and Lathree and Snowball long gone. I loved that hair but the crying it was too much.

Over the water, a cloud of glitter and cackle: light and sound say to gravity: "no," then "perhaps," then "all right, for a while," because the pull of the lovely earth is for a moment greater than the eros of flight. Landing together, all in something of a dither—it's the end of the day and they're hungry—the cranes bustle, then plunge and droop over the icy water, wings cupped under at the tips. Strange appendages, those stick legs, so tidily tucked in flight, drop down for the kerplop into the generous marsh. Finally, a settling, the "aaahh" of tens of thousands of wings folding in one long drawn-out breath: a sigh.

Too fair and all those freckles you had freckles everywhere even on your toes. If I sat you in the sun and made you be still I could even watch them rise to the sweet baby flesh one by one till they filled up your whole face so that it looked like a risen loaf after you dust it with flour or like that moment when the sky gets thick and dark and the birds hush their chatter and the pieces of white fill up the air and you feel them touch you like children touch, wanting to melt into your skin and fold back to the beating heart. You feel them play in the nest of your hair and then you know that the snow has finally come.

XI

Tuesday December 16, 1930
Just 10 more days till Christmas! It snowed hard today. It was realy snow too. You bet it was! And I sure was glad to see it. Goodbye until sometime tomorrow.

Wednesday December 17, 1930
I got a letter from Larthoree today and I sure do wish that she could come home for Christmas. I don't have a thing more to say so thats all for tonight.

Saturday December 20, 1930
Just five more days until Christmas. I haven't had a chance to write anything since Wednesday. Goodbye until tomorrow.

ACKNOWLEDGMENTS

I owe a great debt of gratitude to Louis Gwin, who helped me see my way through this story while it was happening.

I also especially wish to thank Susan Dever, Nancy Gage, Julie Mars, Judith L. Sensibar, Carolyn Woodward, and the anonymous reader for precise, instructive readings of this manuscript. I am deeply grateful for your generosity and creative energies. You are embedded in this book, and it is far the better for your presence.

For encouragement and advice on this project, I am grateful to Marleen Barr, Angela Boone, Barbara Byers, John Crawford, Carol Gwin, Joy Harjo, Lynn Holland, Greg Martin, Deborah McDowell, Margaret Randall, Diana Robin, Julie Shigekuni, Pat Smith, Sharon Warner, Marta Weigle, and Jaimee Wriston Colbert.

My appreciation also goes to John Easterly and Sylvia Frank Rodrigue at Louisiana State University Press for their pivotal decisions and vision concerning the manuscript. I feel very fortunate to have worked with you on this project. I am grateful as well to George Roupe for the balance of care and respect you brought to the editing of this book.

And thank you, Ruth, for saying, yes, write it, sit down and write it.

❊ ❊ ❊

Excerpts from *Wishing for Snow* were previously published as "Decline and Fall: An Excerpt," in *Women's Review of Books* (July 1999), and as "Hearing My Mad Mother's Voices," in *Southern Mothers: Fact and Fictions in Southern Women's Writing,* ed. Nagueyalti Warren and Sally Wolff (Louisiana State University Press, 2000).

Poems by Erin Clayton Pitner were published in *Stones and Roses,* ed. Minrose Gwin (Chamisa Press, 1993). Some of the poems from *Stones and Roses* that are included, in whole or in part, in the present volume, first appeared in the following periodicals and volumes, sometimes in slightly different form or with different titles: *Arulo!:* "Daughter's Lament"; *Attention Please:* "A Rainy Day at Rockport," "Sunday at the Hospice with My Mother"; *The Cape Rock:* "For a Friend Dying"; *Dragon Fire, Dancing Dogs, and Dangling Dreams:* "Night Song"; *Dreaming the Dawn:* "A Word to Wallace Stevens," "Yang or Yin"; *Involvement:* "The Diffident Forsythia," "Dilemma," "The Lost Children," "Mirror of Remembrance," "Mississippi Moon," "My Mother's Room," "Your World and Mine"; *Lyric Mississippi:* "Another World," "For a Friend Dying"; *Mirrors of the Wistful Dreamer:* "Second Blooming"; *Northwoods Journal:* "New Parking Lot"; *The Poet:* "Another World," "Beethoven," "For Erin in August," "I Heard the Children," "Impressions"; *Prophetic Voices:* "In Pursuit of the Dream"; *Shilombish:* "Mirror of Remembrance"; *Texas Review:* "On the Death of a Bluejay"; *Then and Now:* "Cortege," "The Ingathering"; *Voices International:* "Apples in October," "Memento Mori."

"Apples in October," "To a Child on Her Sixth Birthday," and "Wind Child" also appeared in *Mississippi Writers: Reflections of Childhood and Youth,* vol. 3, *Poetry,* ed. Dorothy Abbott (University Press of Mississippi, 1988).

ALSO BY
MINROSE GWIN

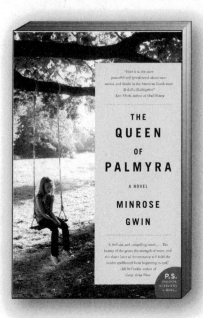

THE QUEEN
OF PALMYRA
A Novel

**ISBN 978-0-06-184032-6
(paperback)**

"Definitely an original. It's darker
than [*The Help* and *To Kill a
Mockingbird*], with a portrait
of Southern race relations that's
more complex and . . . more
accurate than many fictional
depictions."

—*Charlotte Observer*

"Here it is, the most powerful and also the most lyrical novel about
race, racism, and denial in the American South since *To Kill a
Mockingbird*. . . . A story about knowing and not knowing, *The Queen
of Palmyra* is finally a testament to the ultimate power of truth and
knowledge, language and love."

—Lee Smith, author of *On Agate Hill*

"The beauty of the prose, the strength of voice and the sheer force of
circumstance will hold the reader spellbound from beginning to end."

—Jill McCorkle, author of *Going Away Shoes*